Praise for T[...]

"Grief and gratitude are not a dichotom[...] wisdom and emotional intelligence, Lynne Baab invites us to identify the breadth and intensity of our grief *and* gratitude. Drawing on Psalms, Paul, Jesus and his disciples, alongside deeply personal examples of grief and opportunities to exude gratitude, Baab navigates a way for the soul to move beyond cynicism, inadequacy, materialism and denial. *Two Hands* is a delightful book in pandemic times to read prayerfully and contemplatively and in conversation with trusted friends."
—Rev. Dr. Darren Cronshaw, Professor of Missional Leadership at Sydney College of Divinity and Pastor of Auburn Baptist Church

"Lynne M. Baab's graceful, grace-filled Bible study, *Two Hands: Grief and Gratitude in the Christian Life*, offers heartfelt companionship to those who grieve—perhaps a loss or a failing—and give thanks, whether to a person or to God. Lynne's vulnerable sharing of her own experience and her gentle, probing reflection questions at the end of each chapter will help readers claim her wise insights for themselves. *Two Hands* both acknowledges life's challenges and invites us to live more faithfully, authentically, and joyfully with the God of compassion at our side."
—Rev. Dr. Beth Ann Gaede, editor of *When a Congregation Is Betrayed: Responding to Clergy Misconduct*

"Should you ever have the pleasure of meeting Lynne Baab in person, you will experience that all-too-rare-joy of someone *truly* listening to you and understanding you. You will experience that joy in this book. Through a beautiful combination of biblical reflection, personal vulnerability, prayerful engagement, and everyday examples, Lynne guides readers in their own reflection of their own life. You will find yourself in safe hands, revealing you are in God's hands. You will find yourself in Christ."
—Rev. Dr. Geoff New, author of *Echoes: the Lord's Prayer in the Preacher's Life*.

"'We grieve because we love,' writes Dr. Lynne Baab, once again offering welcome wisdom and compassion to followers of Jesus. Drawing on Scripture, the author points us to the One who understands and loves us as we care deeply and are moved by both grief and gratitude. Spend time with this book; it will penetrate your heart with grace."
—Susan S. Phillips (Ph.D.), Executive Director of New College Berkeley (Graduate Theological Union) and author of *The Cultivated Life: From Ceaseless Striving to Receiving Joy*

"*Two Hands* affirms our 'both-and' lived reality: we experience both grief and gratitude, even simultaneously. Neither need compete with the other: each can be integrated into our whole. Drawing on Scripture and personal experience, and offering devotional thoughts and reflections, Baab invites readers to examine their own lives, attentive to the presence of both grief and gratitude. While it can be read alone, *Two Hands* is ideally suited to being explored in the company of others."
—Dr. Lynne Taylor, Somerville Lecturer in Pastoral Theology, University of Otago

"*Two Hands* paints the beautiful and broken picture of our utter dependence on God. When we embrace God's unexpected gifts of grief and gratitude, we learn more deeply of his presence and his loving invitation for connection. As always, Lynne writes in a way that blends theology with practicality to better equip us for a thoughtful life of faith."
—Julie White, Executive Director, The Unfolding Soul

"Lynne Baab brings scripture, personal experience, and pastoral wisdom into this excellent short book which holds grief and gratitude together, stretching us larger for life and ministry. Each chapter includes prompts for prayer, discussion, or reflection suited to Lent or Advent or everyday reading. I hope the book will be widely used."
   —Rev. Dr. Jill Firth, co-editor of *Grounded in the Body, in Time and Place, in Scripture: Papers by Australian Women Scholars in the Evangelical Tradition*

Two Hands

Grief and Gratitude in the Christian Life

Lynne M. Baab

Cover design by Suzanne Mason
Cover art by Dave Baab

Quotations from the Bible come from the New Revised Standard Version
unless otherwise noted.

Contents

Chapter 1 • Holding Grief and Gratitude in Two Hands

What are the benefits of holding grief in one hand and gratitude in the other as a faithful Christian practice?

Worshippers gather for a 7:00 a.m. service. They hear prayers about the fragility and uncertainty of human life. They participate in a prayer of confession that allows them to acknowledge their self-indulgence, anger, lack of love, and failure to serve God with their whole hearts. They receive God's forgiveness. They are invited to think about ways they might journey with Jesus to the cross over the next six and a half weeks.

The worshippers come forward to receive ashes on their foreheads. They hear the somber words, "Remember that you are dust, and to dust you shall return." Some of the worshippers leave the smudge of ashes on their forehead all day, to remember the beauty and sorrow of this holy day.

So many of the themes of Ash Wednesday blend grief with gratitude. We remember our frailty as humans who live on an increasingly damaged earth, but at the same time we remember the God who created our bodies and all of creation, the One who weaves so much beauty and majesty into all we can see, hear, and taste. This God sustains us and the whole universe.

We remember the beauty of human life: art, science, creativity, intelligence, community, and love. We also acknowledge the deep human brokenness and sin that required Jesus' death on the cross. We grieve that Jesus had to die for us, but we are so thankful he was willing to do it. And we rejoice in the power and freedom of the resurrection of Jesus from the dead, defeating the powers of death, sin, and the devil.

Human life is good and rich and wonderful. Human life is full of pain and sorrow. We grieve, and we are thankful. So many aspects and events of human life hold wonderful and sad components.

Grief in One Hand, Gratitude in the Other

Psychotherapist Francis Weller offers a challenge that is perfect for reflection and exploration in our difficult times. His challenge reflects the themes of Ash Wednesday and also echoes the core of the gospel message. Weller is the author of *The Wild Edge of Sorrow: Rituals of Renewal and the Sacred Work of Grief.* He argues that one of the tasks of maturity is to learn to hold grief in one hand and gratitude in the other. We then strive to allow ourselves to be stretched large by both grief and gratitude. This quotation has been shaping my thoughts for the past two years:

> The work of the mature person is to carry grief in one hand and gratitude in the other and to be stretched large by them. How much sorrow can I hold? That's how much gratitude I can give. If I carry only grief, I'll bend toward cynicism and despair. If I have only gratitude, I'll become saccharine and won't develop much compassion for other people's suffering. Grief keeps the heart fluid and soft, which helps make compassion possible.
>
> —"The Geography of Sorrow: Francis Weller on Navigating Our Losses[1]

The Bible is full of this balance between grief and thankfulness. Psalm 103 is an excellent introduction to the presence of both grief and thankfulness in the Bible. It encourages us to think about the brevity and

---

[1] Tim McKee, "The Geography of Sorrow: Francis Weller on Navigating Our Losses" in *The Sun Magazine* (October 2015), https://www.thesunmagazine.org/issues/478/the-geography-of-sorrow (accessed September 19, 2021).

fragility of human life: "As for mortals, their days are like grass; they flourish like a flower of the field; for the wind passes over it, and it is gone" (verses 15 and 16). We grieve that our lives are so short, but "the steadfast love of the LORD is from everlasting to everlasting" (verse 17). The psalm mentions diseases, the oppressed, human sin and transgression (verses 3, 6, 10, and 12), sources of grief for humans everywhere. While the psalm refers to the fragility and brokenness of human life, the majority of the verses of the psalm affirm God's steadfast love in the midst of human life.

Grief comes into particular focus in two seasons of the Christian year, Advent and Lent, which have traditionally been called "penitential seasons." Looking specifically at penitence is helpful because of the word's unique emphasis. *Penitence* is closely related to *repentance*, and the two words are often used interchangeably. The slight difference between the two words is relevant for everyday Christian life. Penitence is connected with regret, while repentance involves turning around, changing course, and starting a new life.

God invites us to reflect on our own sins, which we can confess to God and for which we can receive forgiveness. The gospel of Jesus Christ invites us to repent, which includes turning around and starting afresh after we receive forgiveness. God's grace to us never fails, and in the midst of our sadness for our own brokenness and disobedience, we can give thanks to God, "who redeems your life from the Pit, who crowns you with steadfast love and mercy" (Psalm 103:4).

Penitence—or regret—is a first step toward repentance. We can also feel enormous regret for things that result from human sin and that we have no control over, including other people's destructive actions that often leave a long trail of damage. In addition, we grieve about things that we can do nothing to change, such as illnesses and natural disasters. We cannot turn around or change course personally and have any impact on

8

many of the things that make us sad. The penitence stressed in Advent and Lent enables us to grieve about those situations, including our own powerlessness to change the world.

The grief that Francis Weller describes contains both penitence and repentance. Sometimes we grieve the things that we have done wrong that have resulted in pain for ourselves or others. Sometimes we grieve the human propensity to sin—visible in us and in others—that causes so many negative outcomes. Sometimes we grieve things that are beyond human control.

Linking Grief and Gratitude

You might find that sometimes you experience both sadness and thankfulness related to the same event. Perhaps you've experienced a death in your extended family, and while you and other family members are grieving, you are also grateful for the medical care you witnessed. In that instance, the grief and gratitude are linked in the same situation. In the same way, perhaps a friend or family member lost their job. You are sad and upset in solidarity with the person you love, but at the same time you see ways God provided for them unexpectedly. In addition, maybe you always thought their job was a bit toxic, so you are glad they'll have the chance to explore new options.

Sometimes our grief and thankfulness coexist in different parts of our lives. Maybe an extended family member is extremely challenging for you. You try so hard to act in love and also have appropriate boundaries. You grieve about this uncomfortable relationship, but at the same time you take comfort in a strong and congenial partnership with a colleague. You're grateful for a healthy relationship in a completely different arena of life.

Perhaps right now your grief and gratitude focus on your city or region. Industries grow and decline, housing prices fluctuate, and the number of people who experience homelessness increases. All of these painful situations accelerated during the pandemic. You may be thankful for aspects of your home, neighborhood, and city while also grieving about challenging societal issues.

You may feel some of the same emotions when considering your nation and the whole world. In some instances we grieve over things that we wish politicians could do differently, and in other cases we grieve over viruses, fires, earthquakes, hurricanes, and tornadoes that no one can control. We may simultaneously be thankful for the energy of human response in so many disasters. Effective actions in government—locally, nationally, and internationally—may seem few and far between, but sometimes leaders act in amazing and helpful ways, and we can give thanks to God for them.

You may also want to consider the role of grief and gratitude related to the beautiful earth and universe God created. The press has highlighted recent research showing the healing power of nature, and nature was a lifeline for many during the pandemic. Many Christians experience God's beauty and majesty in nature. We have so much to thank God for: leaves, flowers, trees, skies, rolling hills and mountains, rivers, lakes, and oceans. Our pets and other animals can lift our hearts to God, and the beauty of a child's clear eyes and flexible limbs can brighten our whole day.

At the same time, environmental damage can evoke such deep grief. Everything from chemicals in our air to plastic in the bellies of seabirds arouses deep pain. Rising temperatures worldwide are raising sea levels and increasing the severity of wildfires, which are wiping out islands and damaging huge swaths of forest. While we weep with frustration and grief about damage to the intricate and complex world God made, we hold that grief in tension with our gratitude for the sheer wonder at the beauty of the earth and sky.

That same powerful grief and deep gratitude are very real for anyone who loves the church of Jesus Christ. The wonderful gifts of Christian fellowship and corporate worship are a foundation for many Christians, while the dysfunction of many churches and their leaders causes deep sorrow.

One more area to explore is the role of grief and gratitude in our own personal history. I grieve about decisions I made many years ago that still have a negative impact on my life. At the same time, I thank God for healing, growth, and joy. I grieve the effects of aging in my body, while I am grateful for family and friends and the wisdom that comes with older age. I am thankful for productive work, but I grieve that I have less energy to do it well.

The Bible invites us to reflect on our own sinfulness and to receive forgiveness. I grieve that I have to do this over and over, yet I thank God for grace that flows into my life like a river and never runs out.

Grief and Thankfulness in God's Presence

This journey of holding grief and gratitude in two hands, and allowing ourselves to be stretched large by them, rests on two key truths. The first relates to grief. When we are sad, we do not grieve alone. Jesus is often called "a man of sorrows, and acquainted with grief" (Isaiah 53:3 KJV). He cried over the reluctance of Jerusalem to see what God was doing (Luke 19:41–44). When Jesus approached the tomb of his good friend Lazarus and saw Lazarus's sister Mary weeping, Jesus joined her in her tears (John 11:32–35).

We are not alone in our sadness. If we slow down and let ourselves grieve, we can experience the companionship of the One who cried with his friend Mary and who agonized as he approached his own death (Luke 22:39–46). If we share our sorrows with helpful friends and family members, we will receive companionship from others walking the journey with us.

It may require some effort to figure out who those safe and helpful friends and family members are. Most of us have people in our relationship circles who don't want to grieve with us and who will either push us toward instant optimism or draw us into their own sadness. My prayer for each person reading this book is that you will find people with whom you can share your grief.

I have just described the first foundational idea for this book, that we are not alone when we grieve. A second foundational concept also relates to our connections with God and people: thankfulness nurtures relationships. Much of the writing about thankfulness, increasingly common these days, focuses on having a grateful attitude. An "attitude of gratitude" is definitely good for us and helps us see our world with hope and expectation. However, in the Bible the main point of gratitude is to thank someone, sometimes a human being who has helped us but more often God.

"Bless the LORD, O my soul, do not forget all his benefits" (Psalm 103:2). Don't forget to thank God for the gifts you see and appreciate. Thankfulness turns us toward the person we are thanking, so thankfulness nurtures connection. David Steindl-Rast, in his beautiful book *Gratefulness, the Heart of Prayer*, explains the link that thankfulness creates. "When I acknowledge a gift received, I acknowledge a bond that binds me to the giver. . . . The one who says 'thank you' to another really says, 'We belong together.' Giver and thanksgiver belong together."[2]

When we thank a family member for a gift, a friend for a favor, or a host for a meal, we are saying, "We belong together." When we neglect to

---

[2] David Steindl-Rast, *Gratefulness, The Heart of Prayer: An Approach to Life in Fullness* (Mahwah, NJ: Paulist Press, 1984), 15–17.

thank someone who has helped us in some way, we are missing an opportunity to affirm our connection with that person.

In the same way, thanking God affirms that we belong to God and want to be connected to God. Our bond with God has so many components to it. God made us, and we can express thanks for our bodies, the unique gifts in our personalities, and our inner spirit and soul , which enable us to approach God. God placed us in families and communities. In addition, God made this beautiful earth that we get to enjoy. God came to earth in Jesus Christ and walked in our world. Jesus gave us teaching and a model for so many aspects of how to live. All of these are fuel for thankfulness.

Yes, an attitude of gratitude is a good thing, but even better is thanking actual people and thanking the God of all good gifts. I invite you to embrace this kind of thankfulness and hold it in one hand, with grief in the other hand.

Why I Wrote This Book

In September 2019, I came across the quotation from Francis Weller about holding grief and gratitude in two hands. I was immediately drawn to the picture evoked in my mind: one person holding two things that I had always viewed as totally separate. Sure, the two things were in different hands, showing some distinction and distance between them, but one person is holding both of them. This picture helped me integrate parts of my life that I hadn't been able to hold together.

I was raised in a family where optimism and having an upbeat attitude were prized above all else. Sadness was a "problem," and the worst thing my parents could say about someone was "they have problems." In my adult life I couldn't sustain a high level of optimism, especially after I experienced a rare B vitamin shortage that caused depression. The depression began in my first pregnancy, when my body rightly sent my B vitamin stores to the baby boy growing inside my body, and ended when my older son was 15 and I stumbled into a B vitamin supplement. Only later did I learn that a B vitamin deficiency can be an unusual but real cause of depression.

Throughout my depression and afterwards, I saw my propensity for sadness and the optimism of my family as two approaches at war with each other. I developed a Christian spirituality based on honest expression of emotions. I loved psalms that express sadness or other "negative" emotions, and I often played hymns and praise songs in a minor key on the piano. More than 20 years ago, my husband and I developed a shared practice of thankfulness prayers that spilled over into my personal prayers. Choosing thankfulness has been transformative. But I still couldn't integrate my commitment to honesty about sadness with the healing benefits of watching for things to be thankful for.

In 2019, a month after I found the quotation about holding grief and gratitude in two hands, I began writing a series of blog posts on that topic. I found that writing the posts was personally enriching for me, helping me to evaluate some of the messages from my childhood in the light of my lived experience. Then came the test—the pandemic. Trying to hold sadness and grief in one hand while holding thankfulness in the other hand was the single most helpful strategy I engaged in during 2020 and 2021—lifegiving but also very challenging. Grief hurts, no matter how much thankfulness we can practice alongside it. Grief and gratitude don't cancel each other out. We can learn to hold both of them.

As I began to put together the material for this book, I knew I wanted to explore parts of the Bible that vividly affirm both grief and gratitude: the Psalms, the teaching of Jesus and Paul, and Jesus' last week on earth and journey to the cross. Three of the following chapters—chapters 2, 4, and 6—cover this biblical material.

The Psalms have been my constant companion in this journey of grief and gratitude. I like to listen to psalms as sung by the Australian band Sons of Korah. Over and over in the past two years, the words to various psalms have stretched me to express grief and to see God's gifts. Chapter 2 gives you glimpses of the psalms that have shaped my prayers.

Chapter 4 explores the way Jesus and the apostle Paul allow grief and thankfulness to stretch them large. As Weller points out, without thankfulness alongside, grief can push us to cynicism and despair. However, without grief, gratitude can become overly sweet and can lack compassion for others' suffering. Jesus and the New Testament writers avoided those pitfalls, and we can learn from them.

Chapter 6 focuses on Jesus' last week before his death and resurrection, the ways we see grief and gratitude in his journey to the cross. We remember that Jesus "set his face to go to Jerusalem" (Luke 9:51) and his own death, despite the pain and sorrow he would face. We look toward Easter, when Jesus triumphed over death. We look further ahead to Pentecost and the sending of the Holy Spirit, who guides and empowers us and enables us to experience God's presence with us. We thank a person, the Triune God—Father, Son and Holy Spirit—for such amazing gifts, while we remember the sadness of Jesus' death on the cross.

I structured this book to present a back-and-forth rhythm between the Bible and daily life, interspersing the chapters on biblical material with three topics about everyday life. So chapters 3, 5, and 7 bring us back to our own experience.

Francis Weller invites us to be "stretched large" by holding onto grief and gratitude at the same time. In order to let these two forces work in our lives, we have to rest in them a while. Many forces discourage us from sitting with thankfulness and grief. To the extent that our culture affirms an attitude of thankfulness, we are often encouraged to be thankful for what we have achieved, not what God has done.

Our consumer culture encourages us to buy something new when we're feeling sad. The words "shopping therapy" capture our tendency to seek relief from pain through consumption. Chapter 3 explores ways to overcome the strong voices of the advertising media and cultural voices that encourage shopping and self-congratulation.

In order to embrace the lessons from the Psalms, Jesus, and Paul, we need to pause to look inside ourselves. Many of us have inner voices that discourage us from allowing ourselves to grieve. "What's wrong with me," the inner voice might say, "that I can't be upbeat and positive? Stop feeling sad now." Some inner voices tell us that if we let ourselves feel sad, we will fall into a deep pit of sorrow that we'll never get out of. Chapter 5 focuses on how to counter those inner voices so we can let ourselves be stretched large by grief and then let it go, all the while thanking God for good gifts.

Optimism and hope, coupled with thankfulness, play a significant role in many aspects of both mental and physical health, to be sure. The fifth chapter also explores the similarities, differences, and connections between optimism, hope, and gratitude.

In chapter 7, I write about my own personal lessons regarding grief and gratitude. I tell personal stories about my experiences of grief and gratitude, and I describe the tears that have become more frequent. Thankfulness for me has ceased to be tethered to negative self-talk, so I am laughing more. The lessons for me are ongoing and fruitful.

Each chapter is followed by questions for discussion, reflection, and journaling. I hope and pray that this book will be a springboard to some great discussions in small groups, helpful reflection while walking or doing tasks of everyday life, and fruitful journaling.

I also hope and pray that these reflections on grief and gratitude—and the challenges and blessings of holding them in two hands—will stimulate your thinking and your prayers. I hope and pray that this practice will help you, as it has helped me, navigate our complex and challenging world more faithfully and joyfully.

A Prayer

Loving God, we praise you for your presence with us in hard times. We are so grateful, Lord Jesus, that you cried with the friends of Lazarus at his tomb, so we know you cry with us when we are sad. We are also grateful for the many small and big gifts you give us every day. We ask that this book will help us to grow in our ability to grieve honestly and also to see your blessings, for which we are so thankful. Amen.

Questions for Discussion, Reflection, and Journaling

1. Which comes easier for you, grief or gratitude? What are some of the factors that influence that pattern?
2. Can you think of a time when you experienced both grief and gratitude related to the same event or situation? How did that juxtaposition feel?
3. When you think about the things you are typically sad about, which ones feel like they are completely beyond your control? Which ones do you feel partly or wholly responsible for?
4. God is with us when we grieve. Can you think of an instance when you or someone you know experienced that? What difference did God's presence make?
5. In what ways have you seen thankfulness nurture relationships with people and with God?

6. Think of five things you are thankful for today, and spend a few moments thanking God for them. While you are praying, express to God any sadness you feel today.

Chapter 2 • Grief and Gratitude in the Psalms

What can the Psalms teach us about bringing our grief and thankfulness into God's presence?

The Psalms are full of varied emotions. For millennia, they have guided faithful worshippers into prayer. They invite us to bring all emotions into the presence of God, and they move fluidly between grief and gratitude.

The joy, wonder, and enthusiasm for God's goodness expressed in the Psalms has lifted countless hearts over thousands of years. In some instances, the words of praise are statements about God. "O LORD my God, you are very great. You are clothed with honor and majesty, wrapped in light as with a garment (Psalm 104:1, 2).

Some psalms exhort us to come into God's presence with our praise and thanks. An example of that encouragement comes from Psalm 100:4: "Enter his gates with thanksgiving, and his courts with praise. Give thanks to him, bless his name."

In addition to statements and exhortations related to praise and thanks, many psalms describe pain, sadness, anger, and suffering that the psalm writer brings to God. "Out of the depths I cry to you, O LORD" (Psalm 130:1). The wonder and glory of the book of Psalms is 150 prayers, long and short, that express every human emotion imaginable and portray a God who welcomes us to voice those emotions in God's presence.

Grief in the Psalms

The noun "grief" and the verb "grieve" appear only six times in the Psalms. In one instance, the psalmist refers to the way the people of Israel grieved God when they disobeyed him in the wilderness (Psalm 78:40). The other five instances refer to a person feeling extremely sad and asking God for help. Psalm 31:9 gives a vivid picture of the way our eyes feel after a lot of crying and the way sadness affects our whole body: "Be gracious to me, O LORD, for I am in distress; my eye wastes away from grief, my soul and body also."

Psalm 77 begins with nine verses expressing extreme sadness. Verse ten acts as a pivot point between all that sadness and the remainder of the psalm, which recounts God's faithfulness and wonders. The pivot point in verse ten acknowledges that God works in our hearts to change our grief into something else: "And I say, 'It is my grief that the right hand of the Most High has changed.'" Verses 11 to 20 of the psalm lay out many specific ways God has been good to the people of Israel and describe God's power in nature. God receives our grief and changes it into something else, in this case the ability to see God's good gifts.

Psalm 30:5 describes a similar pattern: "Weeping may linger for the night, but joy comes with the morning." One obstacle to letting ourselves feel grief and sadness is the fear that pain will overwhelm us and we will be unable to get out of the dark pit. Many psalms give us a model for feeling and talking about sadness, with the expectation that at the right time, God will change our hearts into joy and the ability to see, once again, God's goodness in our lives.

Psalm 10 has a structure similar to Psalm 77, with concern and pain in the opening verses and praise in the later verses. While Psalm 77 expresses deep sadness from an unspecified cause, Psalm 10 focuses on the psalm writer's frustration that God seems so distant when evil people prosper. The psalm begins with the question, "Why, O LORD do you stand so far off?" The complaint about the wicked continues until verse 12, when the psalmist begs God to "rise up . . . lift up your hand; do not forget the oppressed."

Then verse 14 describes the psalm writer's change in perspective about how God responds to our prayers: "But you do see! Indeed you note trouble and grief, that you may take it into your hands; the helpless commit themselves to you." God does see! What a relief! This enables the psalm writer to continue with words of praise to God that God is king, hears "the desires of the meek" and "will strengthen their heart," and will "do justice for the orphan and the oppressed" (verses 16–18). Numerous psalms in addition to Psalm 10 and 77 have a similar structure: sadness and grief in a few verses followed by thanks and praise in the next verses.

In addition to the five times the words "grief" or "grieve" are used in the Psalms to describe human emotion, many additional passages describe emotions that we associate with grief. In Psalm 13:2, the psalm writer asks, "How long must I bear pain in my soul, and have sorrow in my heart all day long?" In Psalm 25:16–17, the psalmist begs, "Turn to me and be gracious to me, for I am lonely and afflicted. Relieve the troubles of my heart, and bring me out of my distress." Pain, sorrow, loneliness, affliction, trouble, and distress—these are the feelings that accompany grief, and many psalms describe and vividly illustrate these emotions.

Vivid and Helpful Metaphors

As the psalm writers express their deep need for God in the midst of troubling and sad situations, they use evocative metaphors that connect us to powerful thoughts and emotions. "Incline your ear to me; rescue me speedily. Be a rock of refuge for me, a strong fortress to save me" (Psalm 31:2). The rock, refuge, and fortress metaphors are common throughout the Bible as ways to picture God's strength in the midst of challenges.

While we grieve over so many sad things, we are thankful we can come to God as a source of strength, similar to a rock, refuge, and fortress.

Later in Psalm 31, another vivid metaphor is used, this time to describe the person who is hurting: "I have become like a broken vessel" (verse 12). In a time when the pottery containers used for many household tasks were not as sturdy as our dishes today, a broken pot would have been common.

In the psalms that have a pivot point between sadness and trust in God, the second half of the psalm often focuses on God's actions and character. In Psalm 12, after a few opening verses begging for God's help in the face of wicked people who hurt the poor, a metaphorical description of God's goodness comes in verse 6: "The promises of the LORD are promises that are pure, silver refined in a furnace on the ground, purified seven times." God's promises to help us, heal us, and bring goodness into our lives are as valuable as silver that has been highly refined to become very pure. God's promises, rooted in God's character, play a big role in our ability to bring our grief into God's presence. Because of promises throughout the Bible, we expect that the Holy Spirit will meet us in our grief, bring us through it, and help us see clearly that we have things to be thankful for.

This book is grounded in a metaphor, the picture of a person holding grief in one hand and thankfulness in the other. I'll repeat the quotation that inspired this book:

> The work of the mature person is to carry grief in one hand and gratitude in the other and to be stretched large by them. How much sorrow can I hold? That's how much gratitude I can give. If I carry only grief, I'll bend toward cynicism and despair. If I have only gratitude, I'll become saccharine and won't develop much

compassion for other people's suffering. Grief keeps the heart fluid and soft, which helps make compassion possible.
—"The Geography of Sorrow: Francis Weller on Navigating Our Losses"[3]

Weller's metaphor isn't clear about the exact pattern of how we hold grief in one hand and gratitude in the other. He doesn't say whether he expects that we will give equal attention to both grief and gratitude at the same time or if our focus will shift from one to the other. According to the pattern of the Psalms, we move from grief to thankfulness and then most likely back to grief again when another hard or sad thing happens. This pattern in many psalms indicates that we will seldom hold grief and gratitude in two hands equally at any given moment. Instead, one hand or the other will feel heavier. Francis Weller's helpful metaphor shows us that we need not be afraid when we are grieving that we will get stuck there, and many psalms reinforce that truth. God will enable us, sooner or later, to feel the weight of the hand with thankfulness in it. And when we feel thankful and happy, we need not feel guilt that other people are suffering. We can hold our grief for them in our other hand.

Lament

The psalms that move from sadness and grief to praise and thankfulness are called psalms of lament. Scholars differ on exactly which psalms are to be considered psalms of lament, because in many instances part of a psalm will contain an expression of sadness. The two psalms quoted at length earlier, Psalms 10 and 77, are good examples of psalms of lament.

The word *lament* can be used as a noun or a verb, and as a verb it can be used with or without a direct object. The definitions I'm providing are

---

[3] McKee.

a collection of examples from several online dictionaries. Notice the variety and intensity of the definitions and synonyms:

definition of lament as a verb (used with object)
to feel or express sorrow or regret for death or some form of loss, to mourn for or over

definition of lament as a verb (used without object)
to feel, show, or express grief, sorrow, or regret, to mourn deeply

synonyms for lament as a verb
bemoan, deplore, regret, moan, bewail, sob, rue, wail, cry, bawl, hurt, repine, weep, howl

definition of lament as a noun
an expression of grief or sorrow, sometimes crying out passionately, sometimes formal, such as in verse, song, elegy, or dirge

synonyms for lament as a noun
groan, howl, lamentation, moan, dirge, wail

The intensity of emotion expressed in these definitions and synonyms is instructive in a culture that wants to paste over sadness and grief. If howling, moaning, and wailing are something God invites us to hold in one hand, we have a lot to learn. How do we give our friends and family members the space to express that intensity of emotion? How can we grow to accept those intense emotions in ourselves?

Lament in the Psalms covers a multitude of reasons for the sadness, including death, injustice, losses, and frustration. One source of sadness is personal sin, and a handful of psalms—6, 32, 38, 51, 102, 130, and 143—express contrition for sin, with a request for God's forgiveness.

Psalm 86 begins with a request for God's help because "I am poor and needy" (verse 1). Later in the psalm are words that appear many times in the Hebrew Scriptures: "But you, O Lord, are a God merciful and gracious, slow to anger and abounding in steadfast love and faithfulness" (Psalm 86:15; see also Exodus 34:6, Numbers 14:18, Psalm 103:8 and 145:8, and Jonah 4:2).

God's mercy, grace, steadfast love, and faithfulness, described so often in the Bible, are the foundation for our assurance that we are forgiven when we confess our sins. These characteristics of God give us abundant reason to keep one of our hands filled with thankfulness.

One of those characteristics of God's interactions with humans, steadfast love, is a key component in the hand we fill with thankfulness. The Hebrew word *hesed* (or *chesed*) is translated "steadfast love" in the New Revised Standard Version (the translation used in this book for quotations from the Bible), and the word occurs 248 times in the Hebrew Scriptures.

To translate *hesed*, other translations use love, mercy, loving kindness, loving devotion, faithful love, loyal love, and unfailing love. All these words can provide fuel for thankfulness. In the Psalms, the people of Israel are thankful for both God's character and God's actions in response to human need.

Two Hands

Francis Weller recommends letting grief and gratitude stretch us large. The Psalms help us understand how to do that. With respect to grief, sadness, pain, sorrow, loneliness, affliction, trouble, and distress, the psalm writers show us over and over that we can express those emotions to God. When we do, God sees (Psalm 10:14). God sees not only our emotions, but the situations and relationships that have caused our emotions. God changes those emotions into something else (Psalm 77:10) and acts with justice and steadfast love in the situations we are concerned about. The Psalms invite us to let ourselves be stretched by God's invitation to bring all emotions into God's presence in trust and faith that God sees and God will act.

In the Psalms, thankfulness is almost always directed to God. The concept of thankfulness is associated with joy, a sense of being blessed, and the actions and words of glorifying and praising God. The subject matter of thankfulness is often God's steadfast love and deeds or works that flow out of that love.

"The LORD is my strength and my shield; in him my heart trusts; so I am helped, and my heart exults, and with my song I give thanks to him" (Psalm 28:7). Seeing who God is and thanking God are intricately connected. Music may be involved in the thanks, and we will often thank God along with others: "I will give thanks to the LORD with my whole heart, in the company of the upright, in the congregation" (Psalm 111:1).

Because God answers us when we cry out, we respond in thanks. "I thank you that you have answered me and have become my salvation" (Psalm 118:21). In the Psalms, gratitude is always expressed to God, who is full of steadfast love and who answers us when we cry out for help. Gratitude is part of a relationship, and the psalm writers encourage us to keep our eyes open for God's work in the world and in our lives. The Psalms encourage us to be stretched large in our thankfulness, to watch for what God is doing in the world and pay attention to answers to prayer.

The Psalms call us to make music that expresses our thanks and helps us bring our whole beings into God's presence. The Psalms invite us to situate ourselves in the company of others who love God and who are companions with us on the journey of faith. The Psalms speak of God's loving-kindness and steadfast love, and they encourage us to remember who God is so that we can praise and thank God.

The Psalms use powerful metaphors to help us remember God's character and deeds. God is our rock, refuge, and fortress (Psalm 31:2). "The LORD God is a sun and shield; he bestows favor and honor" (Psalm 84:11). God is our shepherd (Psalm 23:1), and God's word is "a lamp to my feet and a light to my path" (Psalm 119:105). The Psalms invite us to ponder vivid metaphors to remember God's goodness.

Many psalms move fluidly between grief and gratitude. Most psalms imply a give and take between these two stances. One hand will be heavier for a while, then the other hand will take precedence.

A Prayer

Creator God, we cannot thank you enough for the creativity and depth of emotion in the Psalms. We love the word pictures, and we long for you to be our rock, refuge, sun, shield, and shepherd when we are troubled and sad. We love the call to praise and thanks, and we long to hear the music of heaven and reflect that joy in our hearts and in our voices. We love that the psalm writers feel the freedom to bring every emotion into your presence, and we rejoice that you turned their sadness into thankfulness, praise, and joy. Their shift of emotions helps us believe that we will not be trapped in sorrow forever. Help us learn from the Psalms to pray more deeply and more honestly. Amen.

Questions for Discussion, Reflection, and Journaling

1. If you've read straight through this book, you have now read the quotation from Francis Weller two times. What jumped out at you as you read it in this chapter?
2. Review the definitions of lament in this chapter. How do you respond to the strength of emotions described?

3. Many lament psalms have a pivot point where God changes the psalm writer's emotions (Psalm 10:14 and 77:10 are examples). What are the places in your life, and who are the people, that have nurtured pivot points for you? What actions, thoughts, or situations have enabled the pivot to happen for you?

4. Consider the possible translations for the Hebrew word *hesed* found so often in the Psalms and in the Bible: love, mercy, loving-kindness, loving devotion, steadfast love, faithful love, loyal love, and unfailing love. Which of those translations speak to you the most? Why? In what settings are you most able to express thanks to God for this amazing trait of God?

5. In what settings in your life do you find thankfulness comes most easily? What habits have made thankfulness easier for you?

6. Think of five things you are thankful for today, and spend a few moments thanking God for them. While you are praying, express to God any sadness you feel today.

Chapter 3 • Overcoming Messages from Our Culture about Grief and Gratitude

What does our culture say about grief and gratitude? How might a Christian respond?

The voices of our culture come in many forms, and one of the loudest is advertising. The constant message—"buy more"—impacts all of us. Buy more shoes, kitchen utensils, sports equipment, jewelry, electronic devices. Sometimes the message of "more" morphs into "upgrade": upgrade your phone, your tablet, your laptop, your car, your house. Sometimes "more" relates to experiences: try a safari, come to Disney World, check out our new menu.

Sometimes the message of "more" relates to luxury. Those advertisement photos that show one couple on a deserted beach at sunset are telling us that if we visit the resort beside that beach, we will experience the luxuries of a peaceful place and a satisfying relationship. All our needs will be met abundantly. Even the advertisements for minimalistic living have an amusing side. To live a simpler life, the advertisements imply, we need to purchase more storage containers or pay for a book or online class.

These messages have deep significance as we consider how to follow the models for prayer in the Psalms. To bring our sad and painful emotions into God's presence, we have to notice those emotions and acknowledge their significance. We have to live with emotions long enough to know what to say about them to God, which is hard to do when ubiquitous "buy more" messages urge us to turn our focus to the excitement of buying something new or engaging in a new and thrilling experience. The advertising culture urges us to jump immediately to another purchase that will help us push away painful emotions without feeling them for very long or figuring out how we want to pray about them.

A Christian response to the advertising culture can include many forms of stopping and paying attention to what we are feeling and thinking, so we can honestly face the realities of our outer and inner lives. The Psalms can help us train our minds and hearts to accept that painful emotions are part of being human. We also need the companionship of others to help us face our grief honestly without leaping to buy something. We need friends, family members, small groups, ministers and congregational leaders, spiritual directors, and counselors who will draw us out when we're sad and help us explore the anger and other roiling emotions that so often accompany sadness.

Cultural Challenges in the Area of Gratitude

The advertising culture is lethal when it comes to learning to hold grief in one hand, because advertisements urge us to leap from feeling bad into shopping. At least this message affirms on some very small level that sad and frustrating feelings exist. With respect to holding thankfulness in our other hand, the influence of the advertising culture is even more pernicious. Advertisements tell us to focus on what we do not have rather than what we have. This change of focus leaves no room for appreciating God's gifts.

I'll give a personal example. I was a stocky adolescent. My best friend in junior high school was two inches taller than I was and weighed ten pounds less than I did. When I look at photos of the two of us from that time, I see two girls on either side of average. She was a slender average girl, and I was a more rounded average girl. We had different body types within the range of normal and healthy, something I can see now with clarity. At the time, however, the comparison brought me deep pain.

One of the contributing factors was *Seventeen* magazine. I pored over the photos of the waif-like models, and I would have given anything to have a different body. Now, decades later, when a clothing advertisement pops up online, I notice the clothes a little bit, but I notice the models' body shape a whole lot more. I feel slammed with a sense of failure because I am not slender.

When I think about the number of times I have felt inadequate because I am not thin—spread over many decades—and compare those times with the instances when I have thanked God for anything about my body, I am deeply ashamed. I have feet and legs that enable me to walk, and those feet and legs were given to me by God. I have eyes that see the beauty of nature, ears that hear music and the voices of friends, a nose that smells fragrant flowers, and hands that feel glorious textures. God gave me eyes, ears, hands, and a nose. I have a digestive system that enables me to gain both nourishment and pleasure from the taste of foods. God gave that digestive system to me.

I have always enjoyed exercising, these days in the form of water exercise, biking, and weight training. How many people actually get pleasure from exercise? How often have I thanked God for my body's enjoyment of exercise? The advertising culture with all those extremely slender models taught me to change my focus from the gifts God gave me in my body to the one thing I do not have and cannot have no matter how hard I try—a slender build. This sad characteristic of my life seems so superficial and trivial, but it is very real to me.

With respect to my body, I hold grief in one hand—sadness for the innumerable moments of self-criticism—and thankfulness that after so many decades, I am slowly learning to be grateful for my body as a gift

31

from God. Despite this progress, I am still too easily hooked by advertisements with photos of slender women. Over and over, I have to return to the truth that God desires me to bring my sadness into God's presence, that Jesus walks with me in my frustration and anger, and that the apostle Paul calls me to joyful thankfulness because of the great gifts of God in the life, death, and resurrection of Jesus.

My way of being affected by clothing advertisements is only one pattern of many. I know people who have gone into debt because of the pressure they feel to have the latest model of phone, laptop, or car. I know people who spend enormous amounts of money and time on home decorating. Others seek adventurous, expensive experiences. Some are susceptible to advertisements for jewelry or pricey home remodels. In this advertising culture, Christians must support each other in discerning how to resist the voices of the advertising culture. At the same time, our supportive friends help us celebrate the joy of a cruise to the Caribbean or the new car as a gift from God and not as a way to cover over sadness about something.

Another challenge regarding thankfulness comes not from the advertising culture but from the business and sports cultures, and possibly many other sources as well. This voice says that everything good we have comes from our own effort, and we should be proud of what we have accomplished. "Great job," we say to say to our children and grandchildren.

I would have enjoyed more praise from my Depression-era, stoic parents, and I work hard to enjoy the praise from people who encourage me for my contributions. I try to praise others. I want to work hard and enjoy compliments for my efforts. But I also want to find that delicate balance point between excessive pride in my own achievements, on one end of the spectrum, and inability to accept a compliment on the other end. The balance point can be found only by acknowledging that our gifts, strengths, and ability to work hard come from God, and we are called to be grateful.

Overcoming Additional Messages about Grief

The emphasis on having an optimistic attitude, so common in so many Western cultures, profoundly influences our ability to embrace thankfulness and grief. (The connections between optimism, thankfulness, and hope will be discussed at greater length in chapter 5.)

This emphasis can influence how we understand the trajectory of grief after the death of a family member or close friend. Feelings of deep grief create some of the same symptoms as major depression: tears, intense sadness, insomnia, changes in appetite, and trouble concentrating. In the same way that optimism is often "prescribed" in ordinary conversations when someone is dealing with depression, people who are grieving a major loss may receive messages that they should "buck up" and think positive.

Expectations about patterns of grief after the death of a family member or friend illustrate societal pressures in our time. In your circle of friends, how long would feelings of sadness after a death be accepted? How much listening would the bereaved person receive after a few weeks? After a few months?

The Māori people of New Zealand and some Pacific Island peoples mark the one-year anniversary of a death by unveiling the headstone. This gives people permission to experience grief throughout the first year, and the ceremony at the one-year mark also allows loved ones to revisit intense sadness. In many settings in Western cultures, feeling deep sadness for even a few months after a death is viewed as bordering on major depression.

We seem to be afraid of grief. We don't want to feel it. Perhaps no one will listen! Perhaps I'll fall into a pit that I'll never come out of! Perhaps

I'll be viewed as less than competent! How much easier to go online and order something new or make reservations for an exciting new experience. Because we fear grief in ourselves, we often have a hard time listening to others express sadness and pain.

One of the most helpful things a friend can do when someone is experiencing grief after a death is to ask the grieving person to talk about the person who died. What did they admire most in that person? What are some favorite memories? This is a gentle way to help them hold thankfulness in one hand. However, we so often don't ask those kinds of questions because we are afraid we might hear expressions of grief as well.

Old Testament scholar Walter Brueggemann writes about the cultural forces of "royal numbness and denial" that encourage us to numb out, ignore pain, and deny that anything is wrong. He believes that our culture encourages us to engage in these patterns especially related to death and suffering. Brueggemann argues that the role of the prophet is to engage "the community in mourning for a funeral they do not want to admit."[4]

Prophets are not the only ones called to help people mourn "for a funeral they do not want to admit." All of us can help our family members and friends talk honestly about the things that we feel sad about, whether our sadness comes from a "big" event like a death or from something that seems like it should be less painful but may actually still hurt a great deal. So often we simply don't want to admit that life hurts, that the world is so broken that we don't have to look very far to find suffering among both humans and animals.

One sad aspect of practicing numbness and denial is that it short circuits the process of God meeting us in our pain. The apostle Paul describes this process:

---

[4] Walter Brueggemann, *The Prophetic Imagination* (Philadelphia: Fortress Press, 1980), 46.

Blessed be the God and Father of our Lord Jesus Christ, the Father of mercies and the God of all consolation, who consoles us in all our affliction, so that we may be able to console those who are in any affliction with the consolation with which we ourselves are consoled by God. For just as the sufferings of Christ are abundant for us, so also our consolation is abundant through Christ (2 Corinthians 1:3–5).

Not only does honesty before God about our grief enable God to console us, honesty in community builds relationships. Paul explains this gift of Christian fellowship: "We know that as you share in our sufferings, so also you share in our consolation" (verse 7). Growing in suffering together, supporting each other, and caring for each other in pain helps each of us experience God's goodness to us. This process is challenging in the light of the powerful consumer culture and the equally powerful emphasis on optimism and self-achievement that we are bombarded with daily.

I thank God for the gift of the Psalms, those powerful prayers that make room for deep sadness about so many things but also present a pattern of thankfulness following grief. Thank God for sending Jesus to us to demonstrate a life of compassion in the face of human pain, to cry real human tears alongside us, and to proclaim the coming kingdom of God in fullness and joy. Thank God for prophets like Walter Brueggemann and the biblical prophets he writes about, who encourage us to be honest about what we are experiencing and bring it all into God's presence in the company of the faith community.

Thank God for the beauty of nature, where we can have an exciting and invigorating experience apart from the consumer culture, often at very little financial cost. One of the striking developments of the past few years is the increasing press coverage of "forest bathing," the Japanese practice of regularly getting out into nature for the purposes of healing.

Some doctors in Japan won't prescribe antidepressants until the person has tried going into a forest twice a week for a month.

The terms "nature bathing" or "nature therapy" might be even more helpful, because a walk through city or neighborhood streets can have many of the benefits of getting into a forest. Flowers, bushes, trees, clouds, and wind soothe us and speak to us of the beauty of the Creator. Being outside can give us space to honestly consider what we're thinking and feeling, to dwell with the sources of grief and gratitude long enough to identify them, then bring them into God's presence.

Freedom

Embracing grief and thankfulness in two hands, while hearing numerous messages not to do so, is quite freeing. We were created for relationship with God, and every time we bring grief or thanks to God, we are living into the pattern we were made for. Every time we take our sadness or anger into a store or online shopping space and try to cover our emotions over with one more purchase, we are pursuing counterproductive behavior. Every time we view grief as something we're doing wrong, we'll find the sorrow and anger keep sneaking back in painful ways.

Welcoming this challenge to hold grief and gratitude in two hands frees us from pretending that everything is okay. Every single person feels sad, angry, or frustrated about some things. In a fallen world, where nothing is the way God planned for it to be, how can we not experience frustration? God knows how we feel. Jesus who wept at the tomb of his friend Lazarus and journeyed to the painful cross understands our sadness and wants us to draw near to him with it. Being honest about grief and bringing it into God's presence enables us to nurture compassion for others who are hurting, as Francis Weller points out: "If I have only gratitude, I'll become saccharine and won't develop much compassion for other people's suffering. Grief keeps the heart fluid and soft, which helps make compassion possible."[5]

At the same time, holding grief and gratitude in two hands enables us to cheerfully and enthusiastically thank God for the blessings that come to us in this beautiful world created by a God of beauty and love. These good gifts coexist with the sources of sadness and discouragement in our lives. If we don't practice thankfulness, we won't see the flowers amid the weeds, and the grief will dominate to the point of cynicism, despair, and ultimately either paralysis or compulsive behavior of some sort. Francis Weller's words are true: "If I carry only grief, I'll bend toward cynicism and despair."[6]

God invites us to the freedom of honestly acknowledging what we're thinking and feeling, and bringing all that into the presence of the One who understands, listens, cares, and helps.

A Prayer

Jesus, you talked about God's care for every sparrow that falls. You know the small and big sources of sadness in our lives. Help us rest in the knowledge that you care. Help us turn away from advertisements and other pressures to cover up our sadness with another purchase. Help us to be honest about sadness while also noticing your gifts in it. Help us slow down and rest in your goodness. Amen.

Questions for Discussion, Reflection, and Journaling

1. Of all the kinds of advertisements you see and hear, which ones are most tempting to you? What do you find most helpful in turning your attention away from advertisements and consumption toward the things you value most deeply?

---

[5] McKee.
[6] McKee.

2. When you hear the phrase "jumping from sadness into buying something," can you think of stories that illustrate those words? How would you evaluate the outcome of those stories?

3. What cultural messages have you experienced related to thankfulness? Which messages do you want to keep, and which ones do you think aren't consistent with God's values?

4. What helps you turn your focus away from what you don't have toward what you do have? What helps you see God's blessings in your life?

5. If you were talking to a child or young teenager about the influence of advertising for a Christian, what would you say? In what ways do you want to live into your words?

6. Think of five things you are thankful for today, and spend a few moments thanking God for them. While you are praying, express to God any sadness you feel today.

Chapter 4 • Grief and Gratitude in the Gospels and Paul's Letters

What can Jesus and the apostle Paul teach us about grief and gratitude?

In the New Testament, the noun "grief" and verb "grieve" are used just under two dozen times. Sadness is portrayed in numerous additional ways. "Gratitude," "thanks," "thankful," and "thankfulness" are used almost 70 times. These two concepts—grief and gratitude—frequently appear separately. In some cases. we can observe both in the same story or passage.

The Gospels record two incidents when Jesus weeps. One of them occurs on Palm Sunday. Jesus enters the city from the east, coming down a long hill with a view of the city spread out before him. As Jesus looks over Jerusalem, he weeps that the inhabitants did not recognize "the things that make for peace. . . . You did not recognize the time of your visitation from God" (Luke 19:22). Jesus grieves over the lack of responsiveness to God's grace that he has seen in his ministry. Jesus' tears reveal the depth of God's love for human beings. The passage doesn't mention thankfulness directly, but Jesus' tears, as a manifestation of his deep love for the people of Israel, call us to thankfulness for God's amazing love.

Several additional descriptions of grief occur in the tumultuous days between Jesus' entry into Jerusalem and his death, and those incidents are the focus of chapter 6, where I explore grief and thankfulness by walking with Jesus to the cross.

Jesus also cried earlier in his ministry when his friend Lazarus died. Children often enjoy memorizing John 11:35 because in many translations it is only two words, the shortest verse in the Bible: "Jesus wept" (KJV, NIV, ESV, and others). The story of Jesus' tears in this incident reveals a complex interweaving of grief and gratitude.

The story begins when Jesus is some distance from Jerusalem. He receives a message from Lazarus's sisters, Mary and Martha, that Lazarus—"he whom you love"—is sick (John 11:3). Jesus lingers two more days there, telling his disciples that Lazarus's illness "does not lead to death; rather it is for God's glory" (verse 4).

When Jesus approaches the village Bethany, Martha meets him on the outskirts of the village to tell him that if he had arrived sooner, Lazarus would not have died. Jesus says that her brother will rise again. Martha affirms that Lazarus will rise in the resurrection on the last day. Jesus then tells Mary, "I am the resurrection and the life. Those who believe in me, even though they die, will live, and everyone who lives and believes in me will never die" (verses 25–26).

Martha goes to get Mary, and when Mary approaches Jesus, she weeps. Other friends are there, weeping, too. Jesus is "greatly disturbed in spirit and deeply moved" (verse 33), and he weeps along with these mourners. Lazarus's friends take Jesus to the tomb. Jesus is still "greatly disturbed" (verse 38), and he asks the mourners to take away the stone. Then he calls Lazarus to come out, and Lazarus does.

No reader can doubt the intensity of Jesus' grief in this story. Mixed into this story of sadness and grief is amazing power and love. We are thankful that we see Jesus weeping with others, expressing sadness with such openness, solidarity, and care. We are grateful for the model of friendship we see between Jesus and the three siblings, Lazarus, Mary, and Martha.

We also note that Jesus had a significant theological conversation with a woman, Martha, something amazing in his time and a wonderful precursor to the role that women will have in ministry in the future. I am deeply thankful for Jesus' profound and respectful interactions with women.

We rejoice that Jesus not only engages emotively with the needs, feelings, and minds of his friends, but he raises Lazarus as a sign that Jesus himself is "the resurrection and the life" (verse 25).

In neither instance when Jesus weeps does he apologize for the tears or indicate in any way that sadness shouldn't be expressed. He stands in the Jewish tradition, where lament prayers from the Psalms draw people into honesty before God. Jesus is expressing lament through his tears. In addition, his words and actions give us so many things to be grateful for. Grief and gratitude can stretch us large if we ponder this story.

Grief, Anger, and Thankfulness

A story from the Gospels that blends thankfulness and grief even more directly occurs when Jesus enters a village and ten lepers approach him. They keep their distances, as is required by the law, but they call out to him, "Jesus, Master, have mercy on us!" (Luke 17:13). Jesus tells them to go and show themselves to the priest, which was required for healed lepers to be restored to their families. As the lepers walk away, obeying Jesus' words, they are cleansed from the leprosy.

Only one of them, however, seeing the healing of his body, expresses praise to God and turns back to thank Jesus effusively, falling at Jesus' feet. Then Jesus asks, "Were not ten made clean? But the other nine, where are they?" (verse 17). Then I imagine the tone of Jesus' voice when he asks those two questions, I hear a hint of anger, along with a lot of sadness.

How can it be that only one leper, and a Samaritan at that, expresses thanks? This incident mirrors Jesus' tears over Jerusalem, where we see his sadness at the unresponsiveness of the people of Israel. The fact that the thankful leper is a Samaritan reveals that Jesus' ministry extends beyond the bounds of the Jewish community. Jesus is undoubtedly grateful for the response of this Samaritan man, while grieving—and feeling a bit angry—that the other nine, presumably members of people of Israel who were taught for millennia to know God, would accept a gift from God without ever thanking the Giver.

The connection between anger and grief—coupled with a call to thankfulness—is also visible in the incident when Jesus heals a man with a withered hand. Jesus' recent teaching has alerted the Jewish leaders that Jesus has a perspective on the Sabbath different from theirs. When Jesus enters a synagogue on the Sabbath day, the Pharisees are watching him to see if he will do anything they view as unlawful. Jesus calls forward a man with a withered hand, and asks, "Is it lawful to do good or to do harm on the Sabbath, to save life or to kill?" (Mark 3:4). No one responds, and Jesus "looked around at them with anger; he was grieved at their hardness of heart" (verse 5). Jesus then heals the man, and the Pharisees begin to plot with followers of Herod to destroy Jesus.

Jesus' grief at their hardness of heart is mingled with anger. He wants to give life; the Pharisees want people to obey rules, particularly rules related to the Sabbath. We can grieve along with Jesus when religious leaders bring harm to others, rather than enabling goodness and wholeness. We can rejoice in the compassion of Jesus here, a compassion that extends to all who are wounded. We can also ponder the connections between anger and grief.

Grief at the Challenges of Discipleship

Matthew, Mark, and Luke record an incident when a rich man comes and asks Jesus what he must do to inherit eternal life. In Luke, the man is called a "ruler" (Luke 18:18), and in Matthew we learn that he is young (Matthew 19:20). All three gospels record that Jesus responds to the young ruler's question by mentioning the Ten Commandments. The man replies that he has kept these commandments since his youth. Mark records that "Jesus, looking at him, loved him" (Mark 10:21). Jesus tells the man to sell his possessions, give the money to the poor, and come and follow him.

The man, hearing these words, "was shocked and went away grieving, for he had many possessions" (verse 22). What would have happened if the man had said to Jesus, at that moment or perhaps later, "I need help to do that"? What would have happened if the man had brought his grief and sadness to Jesus, as we see modeled in so many psalms? The man's grief juxtaposed with Jesus' love for him creates a fascinating picture of the challenges of discipleship. This story calls us to grieve when we see family and friends walking away from Jesus because discipleship is hard, and Jesus' love for the man in the story calls us to thankfulness.

In four of his letters (Ephesians, Philippians, Colossians, and Thessalonians), the apostle Paul writes out his prayers. The prayer in Colossians echoes the rich young ruler's awareness that discipleship is costly. Paul prays that the Colossians may "be made strong with all the strength that comes from his glorious power, and may you be prepared to endure everything with patience, while joyfully giving thanks to the Father" (1:11, 12). Praying for strength, patience and endurance implies that those characteristics will be needed. The life of discipleship is full of challenges and difficulties. We grieve at the challenges we face in our own personal journeys of discipleship, and we grieve at the difficulties faced by others as they seek to follow Jesus.

Paul goes on to encourage the Colossians to give thanks to God, who "has rescued us from the power of darkness and transferred us into the kingdom of his beloved Son, in whom we have redemption, the forgiveness of sins" (verses 13, 14). This passage is one of many in Paul's letters where he expresses his joy, wonder, and gratitude for God's gift of grace through Jesus Christ. Paul stands in awe of the magnificence of God's gift and calls us to stand in awe, with thankful hearts.

All the prayers Paul records abound with thankfulness for God's work in the believers, whom Paul loves and to whom he is writing. "I thank my God every time I remember you," he writes to the Philippians (1:3). To the Thessalonians he says, "We always give thanks to God for all of you . . . remembering before our God and Father your work of faith and labor of love and steadfastness of hope in our Lord Jesus Christ" (1 Thessalonians 1:2, 3). When we see God's work in our brothers and sisters, we are called to thankfulness.

The letter to the Ephesians contains two prayers. The prayer in the first chapter (verses 15–19) is similar in structure to the prayer in the Colossians. Paul begins with thanks for the Ephesians, prays that they might grasp the riches God has given them, and then expresses his wonder at the work of God in Christ (verses 20–23).

The prayer in Ephesians 3 reflects Paul's awareness of what Christians need in order to be faithful disciples in a challenging world. He prays that "you may be strengthened in your inner being with power through his Spirit, and that Christ may dwell in your hearts through faith, as you are being rooted and grounded in love" (verses 16 and 17). His words acknowledge the need for strength in the face of the difficult situations we face, as well as the love we need in an often loveless world. We grieve about difficulties and lack of love, we pray for God's help, and we give thanks that God gives it.

Anger Plus Grace in Galatians

In several of his letters, Paul addresses specific concerns he knows about in the churches he is writing to. In 1 Corinthians, he talks about divisions and sexual immorality in the Corinthian church and expresses his deep concern—even grief—for the ways the Christians there are not following Christ. In Galatians, Paul's language of confrontation is even more powerful. For example, in Galatians 1:3 he writes, "I am astonished that you are so quickly deserting the one who called you in the grace of Christ and are turning to a different gospel." The words "astonished" and "deserting" convey intensity of feeling. Paul is upset at a level that can be described as grief.

The Galatians have apparently reverted to trying to earn God's approval through obedience to the Old Testament law. Various teachers, Paul says, "are confusing you and want to pervert the gospel of Christ" (1:7). He asserts that "if anyone proclaims to you a gospel contrary to what you received, let that one be accursed!" (1:9). He cries out: "You foolish Galatians! Who has bewitched you?" (3:1). Again, notice the vividness of the words "pervert," "accursed," "foolish," and "bewitched." Paul is expressing his passionate sadness, even anger, through this evocative language.

In Galatians, Paul writes a great deal about freedom and slavery. In fact, "slave" and "slavery" are used 19 times in the letter. The false teachers, Paul says, "slipped in to spy on the freedom we have in Christ Jesus, so that they might enslave us" (2:4). He summarizes his teaching about freedom and slavery: "For freedom Christ has set us free. Stand firm, therefore, and do not submit again to a yoke of slavery" (5:1).

Paul adds two twists to his teaching about freedom and slavery. Not only are we called to freedom, but in Christ all barriers are broken: "There is no longer Jew or Greek, there is no longer slave or free, there is no longer male and female; for all of you are one in Christ Jesus" (3:28). The freedom Christ brings us allows us to see people through vastly different lenses.

His second twist is equally challenging. "For you were called to freedom, brothers and sisters; only do not use your freedom as an opportunity for self-indulgence, but through love become slaves to one another" (5:13). Instead of being enslaved to the law, Paul wants us to be enslaved to each other as willing servants who love and care and bear each other's burdens (6:2).

The book of Galatians describes the challenges of discipleship. We so easily fall into slavery to rules and standards, instead of relying on God's grace. We have such a hard time seeing the equality of people with a different ethnicity, socioeconomic status, and gender. Equally hard is serving each other with the strength of Christ's love; divisions and conflict in the church are all too common. Along with Paul, we grieve how often we fall short as we strive to live by the grace of Christ. But also along with Paul, we thank God for the freedom we have received in Christ and the guidance and strength to follow Jesus' model in serving and loving others.

Jesus and Paul unapologetically model sadness and grief, and they show us that anger is often a component of grief. Both Jesus and Paul call us to the challenges of faithful obedience to God, knowing how hard and yet rewarding it will be. Jesus and Paul also call us to give thanks for all of God's goodness. They show us how to hold grief in one hand and gratitude in the other. They are stretched large by both, and they invite us to the same experience. We grieve with Jesus and with Paul for so many aspects of human life. And, at the same time, we rest in God's goodness to us through Christ.

A Prayer

Jesus, our Savior and Friend, thank you for your tears. Those tears teach us so much about your heart for us. Give us the tenderness of heart that enables us to weep for injustice, lack of love, and human pain. Thank you for Paul's prayers that help us see the challenges and costs of discipleship. We grieve at the challenges of following you, but we are so grateful you have called us to be your disciples and friends. Help us to be stretched large by your model of living with grief and gratitude, as well as your model for all of life. Amen.

Questions for Discussion, Reflection, and Journaling

1. When you think of favorite passages in the Bible about grief and about gratitude, what comes to mind?

2. When you think of Jesus' interactions with people, where do you see Jesus' sadness? Where do you see his thankfulness to his Father or to people?

3. Which Gospel stories make you thankful for Jesus? Which of Jesus' personality traits and actions are you most grateful for?

4. Being a faithful disciple of Jesus is challenging. Which challenges make you grieve for yourself and for others? In what ways are you grateful for challenges?

5. Galatians focuses on freedom in Christ. What are you grateful for related to the freedom you experience through Christ? Do you ever experience sadness as you face the challenges of living out that freedom?

6. Think of five things you are thankful for today, and spend a few moments thanking God for them. While you are praying, express to God any sadness you feel today.

Chapter 5 • Overcoming Inner Voices that Deny Grief and Gratitude

How might we draw on God's healing and welcome to address the inner voices that shape our understanding of grief and gratitude?

Many lessons from our childhood and family of origin stick with us. Verbal and nonverbal messages from childhood and our teen years turn into inner voices that shape the way we approach daily life. My husband used to spend a lot of time with his father in his workshop, and as they worked on projects together, his dad always said, "You're a finisher, Dave." Those words were a big blessing to Dave. They enabled him to persevere in many areas of life, which led to excellence in his career and as a father and husband. Dave's ability to finish what he starts gives him great satisfaction. However, the words have had a downside. Dave was left with an inner voice that tells him he can never quit anything. He has learned—with a great deal of effort—to pay attention to evidence telling him "this is enough" or "stop now."

My parents valued a practical, problem-solving approach to life, which shaped me into a can-do person. While I appreciate being able to tackle problems, I also remember the painful stage of being awash with teenage hormones. My mother said, "You're so smart. Surely you can figure out how to deal with your emotions." Being told to apply cognition to emotions was truly unhelpful and created lifelong inner voices that have been hard to cope with. My mother's comment came straight out of her own heritage.

My parents were raised during the Depression, when a stoic acceptance of ahard times seemed to most people to be a helpful coping strategy. I don't recall my father ever expressing sadness about anything, even when his own parents died. My mother had a beloved little sister who died when my mother was 12 years old, and after the death, all the relatives told my mother that she needed to take care of her mother. No one expressed any compassion for my mom's own sense of loss.

As might be expected, her own experiences impacted her style of parenting. She seemed deeply uncomfortable with my emotions of sadness and anger, and her most common way of responding was to say, "You're not sad" or "You're not angry." At the same time, I cannot count the number of times I have heard my mother say: "They never encouraged me to grieve with my mother. We should have cried together! Instead, my entire family did everything we could to deny that we were sad." Despite this verbal assent to the significance of grief, the messages from her childhood had clearly taken root.

This pattern from my childhood created deep inner messages that "negative" emotions are not acceptable, and that I should do everything I can to keep them from surfacing. I have had to work very hard to learn to feel and sit with emotions that my mother considered to be negative— sadness, frustration, anger, and grief. I have always found it easier to eat something soothing like cookies or cake when beginning to feel a "negative" emotion rather than to sit with it, allow it to speak to me, and bring it into God's presence.

Your messages from childhood will undoubtedly be different from Dave's and mine. You may have received some gender-based messages that have turned into inner voices. *Men should hide their emotions. A truly feminine woman is caring and gentle and never expresses any anger. Men are supposed to be tough, so anger is okay—but never sadness, tears, or any kind of vulnerability. Women should focus on their appearance and hide their emotions.* Even gender-based assumptions vary from one family to the next, demonstrating the complexity of teasing out the impact of childhood messages.

Some people, both men and women, heard things in childhood and their teen years that led them into "imposter syndrome," a deep-seated worry that they will be exposed as a fraud or incompetent. This creates a constant state of hypervigilance that makes it very difficult to be aware of current thoughts and feelings. The cultural voices explored in chapter 3 often turn into inner voices telling us that when we feel bad, we need to buy something or do something distracting and exciting.

These inner voices can create challenges in the journey toward holding grief and gratitude in our two hands. Many parts of the Bible—as described in chapters 2, 4, and 6—model or encourage an honest approach to emotions. Psychologists tell us honesty about emotions is important because of their significant role in revealing to us what we value. I have tried to embrace that conviction.

Embracing Grief

My first exposure to the freeing idea that God invites us to bring all of our emotions into God's presence—rather than trying to deny them or ignore them or eat cookies to dull their impact—came from the book of Jeremiah. In my early twenties, I came across the prophet's passionate prayers. In one prayer Jeremiah "lays charges" against God because God allows evil people to thrive (12:1). Jeremiah also tells God that God's hand on his life is heavy: "Why is my pain unceasing?" (15:18). He continues, calling God a "deceitful brook, like waters that fail." He curses the day he was born and curses the man who brought the news of his birth to his father (20:14, 15).

As a young adult, coming out of a can-do family where emotions were denied, I was astonished by Jeremiah's passionate expressions of pain. These prayers are in the Bible! Why did my parents, and the churches we attended, ignore these prayers? I felt as if a load had been taken off my shoulders. I didn't have any desire to curse God or call God deceitful. I just wanted to be able to honestly acknowledge what I was feeling and to have the sense that my often intense emotions weren't a sign that something was wrong with me.

The Psalms helped me continue a journey of understanding that God created emotions, welcomes our expression of emotions, comes alongside us when we feel sad and angry, and then enables us to move back to a place of equilibrium and joy. As a young and midlife adult, I hadn't yet come across the metaphor of holding grief and gratitude in two hands at the same time. However, the Psalms facilitated a long journey toward a rhythmical life, moving back and forth between sadness/anger and praise/thanks, bringing all emotions into God's presence.

The life of Jesus as described in the Gospels made an impact as well. Jesus' tears at the death of his friend Lazarus (John 11:28–37) and when he cried over Jerusalem (Luke 19:41–44) had a straightforwardness and honesty that impressed me. The Gospels record no hint that he expressed embarrassment for being "negative" or "too emotional," some of the labels my inner voices tell me to assign to passionate feelings. Jesus' anger when he confronted religious leaders (Matthew 23:1–36) and when he cleared the Temple (John 2:13–22) was also quite thought provoking. I felt angry more often than I wanted to, and I had absorbed some cultural messages about anger being inappropriate for women, so my anger always felt too big. I wasn't sure how to view those stories about Jesus feeling and expressing anger. I told myself that he was the Son of God and knew how use anger in a correct way. As a flawed human being and as a woman who had never seen a woman express anger in any way that seemed productive, I wasn't sure Jesus' model applied to me.

I was in my late thirties when I read a book that changed my perspective on anger—*Anger: The Misunderstood Emotion* by Carol Tavris

(Simon and Schuster, 1989). Tavris argues that without anger, there would be no great social movements—no abolition of slavery, no vote for women, no Freedom Riders fighting for voting rights for African Americans, no Clean Air Act or Clean Water Act. She helped me see that anger helps us identify our values and then find the energy to act on those values. Her book helped me begin to notice the physical signals in my body when I'm angry. For me, anger begins low in my chest and moves upward into my throat, then into my forehead, where it pounds.

I now know that anger is a component of grief, visible in the life of Jesus (Mark 3:1–6; Luke 17:11–19) and in the five stages of grief described by Elisabeth Kübler-Ross. If we're going to grow in our ability hold grief in one hand, then we will have to be honest about the significance of anger in grief.

Kübler-Ross is only one of many researchers in the field of psychology who have given us insights into the role of emotions, including the emotions deemed to be "negative" in my childhood. Her 1969 book, *On Death and Dying* (Simon and Schuster), proposed that people who are dying go through five stages of grief: denial, anger, bargaining, depression, and acceptance. Later research has confirmed the presence of those stages in the experience of grief but not necessarily in that order and not in a linear fashion. Instead, grieving people tend to cycle and swirl among those stages. Those five experiences within grief are also common as we grieve many other losses in addition to death, and other researchers have described additional components.

Moving from the "you're not angry" and "you're not sad" messages that I internalized in my childhood to a stance that welcomes emotions as a source of information and even wisdom has been a long journey for me with many steps still to come. Learning that I can hold grief and gratitude in two hands has been a significant step in leaning into the sadness and anger that accompany grief. The grief doesn't dominate. It is partnered with soothing and uplifting expressions of thankfulness.

Overcoming Obstacles to Thankfulness

In the same way that inner messages impede the ability to embrace grief for many of us, we may have inner messages about thankfulness as well. Many of us grew up in communities where the pioneer lifestyle is only a few generations in the past, and we have been shaped by that fiercely self-sufficient narrative. This view encourages us to think that acknowledging someone has helped us shows that we are weak. In chapter 1, I mentioned the beautiful book *Gratefulness, the Heart of Prayer* by David Steindl-Rast. He argues that gratitude creates a connection between people: "The one who says 'thank you' to another really says, 'We belong together.' Giver and thanksgiver belong together."[7] In contrast to the pioneer mentality, some of us need to affirm to ourselves that gratitude does not indicate weakness. And in reality, even in the pioneering days, people depended on each other in profound ways, and thanking others for the way they helped created a strong bond on the frontier.

Receiving thanks also nurtures that bond. Some of us have internalized messages that keep us from easily accepting the thanks of others. Consider the difference between these two scenarios. In the first scenario, someone thanks you for a small favor. You smile and say, "You're welcome. I'm so glad I could help." In the second scenario, after receiving thanks, you say, "Really, it was nothing. I don't deserve thanks for that small thing." The first response nurtures the relationship, while the second leaves the thankful person a bit confused.

For thankfulness to nurture relationships, we need to make the effort to express thanks in face-to-face conversations, by email, text message, social media, or in a traditional card or letter. We need to accept thankful

---

[7] Steindl-Rast, *Gratefulness, The Heart of Prayer*, 15–17.

words with gratitude that the interchange has nurtured our relationship. And we also need to understand the difference between optimism and thankfulness.

Recent research affirms the value of optimism, which is correlated with resilience under stress, emotional well-being, and solid relationships. We often conflate thankfulness and optimism, but they are not the same thing. Christians who want to feel and express gratitude for God's abundance will find it helpful to tease out the differences.

Combining definitions from online dictionaries, I would describe optimism as "hopefulness and confidence about the future or the successful outcome of something." Hope is a major theme in the New Testament. Paul uses the name "God of hope" in Romans 15:13, and in 1 Corinthians 13:13 he describes faith, hope, and love as things that endure.

So if optimism is composed of hope and confidence, why would we not want to embrace it all the time? An interviewee for my book on Christian pastoral care, *Nurturing Hope* (Fortress Press, 2018), is a psychiatric nurse practitioner. She told me that optimism can be overemphasized. When we focus on optimism too much, she said, we can slide into denial, the refusal to admit the truth or reality of something. Thus, a too-strong emphasis on optimism can impede our willingness to feel grief.

The nurse practitioner said thankfulness can bring about the same good results as optimism in many difficult situations but without denial. Thankfulness is a choice to focus our eyes on good gifts. Those gifts might come from the people around us—a stimulating conversation, an act of kindness, direct help that meets a need, an encouraging word, a doctor or other professional who gives help we need, or many other specific gifts, big or small.

Thankfulness also enables us to see God's good gifts that come directly to us from God—an answer to a prayer, a situation that works out well despite the odds, inner strength to do something difficult, or peace that passes all understanding. Thankfulness also helps us notice the good gifts in the physical world God created—fresh fruit in season, the clear eyes of a child, colorful fall leaves and beautiful spring flowers, a vivid sunset, dramatic mountains, and towering clouds.

Thankfulness creates a foundation for hope. We are hopeful and confident about the future because of God's faithfulness, which we observe in the present as well as the past. We trust in God's promises because, by being thankful, we have schooled ourselves to see the fruit of God's promises.

When we focus on the good gifts that are present in our lives, we do not deny the reality of pain, stress, challenges, and grief. Thankfulness involves turning our eyes to see good things even amid difficulties, and we take a moment to thank the giver of the gift.

Steindl-Rast wonders if our society suffers so much from alienation because we are reluctant to offer thanks. Our friendships and family relationships clearly suffer when we feel uneasy acknowledging bonds with other people, when we hold back from expressing gratitude. He points out that everything is a gift, yet we find it hard to acknowledge gifts because we don't like to admit our dependence.[8] Thankfulness, held in one hand, involves acknowledging that we belong with others and with God and that we depend on the people around us and on God. We are not alone. We are not self-sufficient. We cannot navigate life on our own.

Grief, held in our other hand, can also help us acknowledge that we belong with others and with God. We grieve because we love. We grieve alongside Jesus, the "man of sorrows and acquainted with grief" (Isaiah 53:3 KJV). Our emotions of sadness are a guide to the values that connect us with people, and thankfulness is a joyful way to build connections with people we care about. However, many of us have to work to replace inner

---

[8] McKee.

voices that deny the place of grief and discourage expressions of thankfulness with the freedom to be honest about what we're feeling and seeing.

A Prayer

Creator God, we praise you for the beauty of creation that gives us joy so often. We praise you that you created our bodies, minds, hearts, and spirits. So often we face challenges because of messages and beliefs hidden inside us. Help us perceive the inner forces that make it difficult for us to see good gifts in our lives and thank the giver of those gifts, whether that is a person or you. We ask for forgiveness for our pride in self-sufficiency. We ask for healing of the wounds that keep us from rejoicing in your good gifts and also make us resist heartfelt expressions of sadness and grief. Help us grow in your calling to live as your beloved children. Amen.

Questions for Discussion, Reflection, and Journaling

1. When you look back on your childhood and teen years, how did the people around you react to sadness and anger? Which other emotions were considered negative? Did some of those responses turn into inner voices that influence you today? How have you addressed those inner voices?

2. What did you learn in childhood and your teen years about expressing thanks to people and to God? Describe the positive and negative aspects of what you learned and the way those patterns influence you today.

3. Over the course of your adult life, what practices have you found helpful in challenging and changing inner voices that are not helpful or faithful to God's values?

4. What is the strongest inner message that influences your ability to sit with sadness and grief? In what ways would you like God to change it?

5. What is the most powerful inner message that impacts your practice of thankfulness? Are you happy with it, or do you want to ask God to change it?

6. Think of five things you are thankful for today, and spend a few moments thanking God for them. While you are praying, express to God any sadness you feel today.

Chapter 6 • Grief and Gratitude with Jesus on His Way to the Cross

What do Jesus' last days on earth teach us about grief and gratitude?

We use the terms "Holy Week" or "Passion Week" to describe that eventful, tumultuous, and emotional week that begins with Jesus' triumphal entry into Jerusalem on Palm Sunday and ends with his resurrection. Depending on whether you count words, verses, or chapters, the events of Holy Week take up between one-quarter and one-third of the four Gospels.

We use palm branches and music-filled processions in our congregations to remember Jesus' triumphal entry into Jerusalem, but we seldom focus our attention on the tears Jesus wept over Jerusalem on that same day. "If you, even you, had only recognized on this day the things that make for peace! But now they are hidden from your eyes," he says as he sees Jerusalem and cries. Jesus says that the people of Israel do not recognize "the time of your visitation from God" (Luke 19:42, 44). We can hear grief in his words, and we see grief in his tears.

His sadness mirrors our own sadness when we look at places with an absence of "things that make for peace." Jesus would have been thinking of the Hebrew concept of peace, shalom, which means well-being in every area of life. We grieve with Jesus at the many people who lack economical, relational, and spiritually well-being. We grieve about political and economic forces that do not promote well-being of precious humans who are loved by God. We grieve with Jesus about the areas in our own lives and in the lives of people we love where we do not experience fullness of life. In the same way that Jesus looks over Jerusalem and grieves, we often look at human life and feel a similar sadness.

Jesus' Grief during Holy Week

The Gospels record numerous additional times when Jesus expresses sadness, frustration, anger, and grief in the few days between the triumphal entry and his crucifixion, and much of his grief has significant parallels today. Three Gospels record his criticism of the religious leaders shortly after the triumphal entry, with Matthew giving the most detail. Jesus says, "They tie up heavy burdens, hard to bear, and lay them on the shoulders of others; but they themselves are unwilling to lift a finger to move them. . . . But woe to you, scribes and Pharisees, hypocrites! For you lock people out of the kingdom of heaven. For you do not go in yourselves, and when others are going in, you stop them" (Matthew 23:4, 14). We grieve today about abuse by clergy and other church leaders that profoundly damages many people's ability to see God's kingdom as desirable. We grieve when we see churches laying unnecessary burdens on their members.

Matthew and Luke record Jesus using the metaphor of a hen. Jesus says that he tried many times to gather the people of Israel like a hen gathers her brood under her wings, "and you were not willing" (Matthew 23:37). Matthew also records Jesus' using the metaphor of separating sheep from goats based on whether people fed him, gave him drink, welcomed him, and clothed him (Matthew 25:31–46). These metaphors continue to have power today. We grieve today when we see beloved friends and family members who have no interest in accepting God's love for them, and we grieve at the hard-heartedness we see in Christians—and sometimes in ourselves—when we refuse to provide care for people in need.

Judas's betrayal of Jesus is woven though Holy Week. Early in the week, Judas goes to the chief priests to negotiate the fee they will pay him to deliver Jesus into their hands. All four of the Gospels record Jesus' words at his last dinner with his disciples, when he predicts that one of the twelve will betray him (Matthew 26:21–25). Jesus also predicts Peter's denial. Jesus says to Peter, "Truly I tell you, this very night, before the cock crows, you will deny me three times" (Matthew 26:34). The Gospels do not record Jesus' emotional response to these betrayals by his companions. We can imagine the sadness, anger, and pain that he must have felt, and we can identify with those emotions in the face of betrayal. All too often, we have seen our loved ones betrayed, and we have experienced betrayal ourselves and the deep pain that follows. In addition, many of us can identify moments when we have betrayed others. All of these experiences evoke emotions of deep sadness.

Jesus' most intense expression of emotion comes in the Garden of Gethsemane, where he begs his disciples to stay awake. Matthew describes him as "grieved and agitated" (Matthew 26:37), and Mark uses the words "distressed and agitated" (Mark 14:33). Jesus addresses Peter, James, and John: "I am deeply grieved, even to death; remain here, and stay awake with me" (Matthew 26:28). These are the only verses in the Holy Week narratives where Jesus is described as "grieving," using that specific word.

Matthew, Mark, and Luke record Jesus' pleas and expressions of willingness related to his death: "My Father, if it is possible, let this cup pass from me; yet not what I want but what you want" (Matthew 26:39). Matthew and Mark describe Jesus' words of forsakenness on the cross: "My God, my God, why have you forsaken me?" (Matthew 27:46).

One additional mention of grief comes from Luke, who recounts that when Jesus got up after praying in the Garden of Gethsemane, "he came to the disciples and found them sleeping because of grief" (Luke 22:45). That cryptic comment raises the question of what exactly the disciples were grieving and why their grief would make them sleep. Their sleep and grief in the Garden follow an intense dinner, when Jesus washed their feet and then talked with them about many significant topics, so perhaps their fatigue is understandable.

In addition to the single instance when grief is explicitly attributed to Jesus and the second instance when the disciples slept because of grief, the emotions of sadness, frustration, and anger are portrayed numerous times in the Holy Week accounts. Because those emotions are related to grief, they help us enter into Jesus' grief in the days leading up to his death and into the tumultuous emotions the disciples experienced.

Grief and Gratitude in John 13 to 17

Compared to Matthew, Mark, and Luke, the Gospel of John goes into much more detail about the night that Jesus was betrayed. Four chapters—John 13 to 17—describe the events before, during, and after dinner, often presumed to be a Passover meal. Jesus is with the 12 disciples, and the chapters open with the foot washing and Jesus' prediction that one of the disciples will betray him. Judas leaves. Then Jesus talks to the disciples about numerous topics and prays for them.

The words "grief" and "thanks" do not appear in these five chapters, but when I read the chapters, I find much to be grateful for and much to grieve. I rejoice in Jesus' model of servanthood made visible in the foot washing (John 13:1–17), but I also grieve the many times when I have been unable or unwilling to serve those around me. In the first 14 verses of John 14, Thomas and Phillip ask Jesus questions about how we will know the way to follow Jesus and how we can see the Father. Jesus' answers are beautiful and timeless, a powerful invitation to draw near to Jesus in order to know God more fully. I am so grateful for Jesus' life, death, and resurrection, which make knowing God possible, but I grieve that my knowledge of God is so limited and self-focused.

Jesus' teaching about the Holy Spirit in John 14:14–31 and 16:4–15 lays out the many ways the Holy Spirit leads, teaches, and empowers us. I thank God for Jesus' presence with me through the Holy Spirit, but I grieve that the Spirit's voice is so difficult to hear, and I grieve for all those moments when I just can't find the focus or willingness to rely on the Holy Spirit for guidance. I grieve that Christians disagree among ourselves about what we believe the Holy Spirit is saying to us as individuals and as church communities, and about exactly where and how the Holy Spirit is leading, and I am so sad for those divisions.

Jesus lays out another powerful metaphor—the vine and the branches—in John 15:1–17. The metaphor expresses an invitation to abide in Christ. I am so grateful for the power of the metaphor and for the many times I have been guided and empowered by that vivid picture of vines and branches cared for by the gardener. Jesus is clear as he develops the metaphor that the gardener cuts back living branches so that they can ultimately bear more fruit. Ouch! I grieve for the many times I resist the work of the master gardener in my life. And I grieve for the times I simply don't want to abide in the vine.

John 17 records Jesus' prayer for his disciples—the ones there in the room with him and the ones who will believe later because of the apostles' words. In verse 3, Jesus says, "And this is eternal life, that they may know you, the only true God, and Jesus Christ whom you have sent." I rejoice in the eternal life available in Jesus Christ. I am so grateful we can know God, and I grieve that knowing God is sometimes so challenging. In the next verses, Jesus adds, "I glorified you on earth by finishing the work that you gave me to do." Christians around the world give God deeply felt thanks for Jesus' faithfulness in finishing the work he was called to do, and we grieve that Jesus' obedience was so costly and caused him so much pain.

Jesus' prayer for oneness is one of the most challenging parts of his prayer. Jesus prays, "Holy Father, protect them in your name that you have given me, so that they may be one, as we are one" (verse 11). He repeats that idea later in the prayer: "The glory that you have given me I have given them, so that they may be one, as we are one, I in them and you in me, that they may become completely one, so that the world may know that you have sent me and have loved them even as you have loved me" (verses 22–23). This theme in the prayer echoes his words from earlier that night: "I give you a new commandment, that you love one another. . . . By this everyone will know that you are my disciples, if you have love for one another" (John 13:34, 35). Jesus indicates that our oneness and love as followers of Jesus will be a witness to the world.

Christian worshippers praise and thank God for the oneness and love between the members of the Trinity, and we are so grateful we get glimpses of that love throughout the Bible. But oh, how I grieve that love and oneness are so difficult for me. I grieve at the many examples of Christians' lack of love.

Our call to Christian mission comes from this prayer. Jesus prays, "I am not asking you to take them out of the world, but I ask you to protect them from the evil one. They do not belong to the world, just as I do not belong to the world. Sanctify them in the truth; your word is truth. As you have sent me into the world, so I have sent them into the world" (verses 15–18). I rejoice that Jesus so vividly describes the tension of being in the world but not belonging to it. I rejoice that Jesus gives me, and all Christians, a mission. Our lives have meaning and purpose because we are sent into the world as Jesus was sent. I grieve that living faithfully in the world, and fulfilling the mission Jesus called us to, is so challenging. All too often, Christians have done a poor job of living in the world as Jesus did, and I am so sad about that, too.

Jesus' words to his disciples on that last night before his betrayal and death, and his prayer for them, contain many additional ideas that evoke both grief and gratitude. Jesus' words and his prayer give us a powerful insight into his priorities for his disciples as he approaches his death, and they give us much fuel for both grief and gratitude.

Francis Weller's Two Hands and Holy Week
Here is one last look at the quotation that inspired this book:

> The work of the mature person is to carry grief in one hand and gratitude in the other and to be stretched large by them. How much sorrow can I hold? That's how much gratitude I can give. If I carry only grief, I'll bend toward cynicism and despair. If I have only gratitude, I'll become saccharine and won't develop much compassion for other people's suffering. Grief keeps the heart fluid and soft, which helps make compassion possible.
> —"The Geography of Sorrow: Francis Weller on Navigating Our Losses"[9]

In many ways, Jesus' journey to the cross in the last days of his life illustrates Francis Weller's perspective. Weller says that if we carry only grief, we bend toward cynicism and despair. I don't hear cynicism in Jesus' words in his last week, but I do hear moments of despair. His grief and pain are so intense that thankfulness and joy are mostly crowded out. We acknowledge the reality of times in our own lives when grief takes over, when our pain is overwhelming.

Now, looking back centuries, we are able to rejoice in the empty tomb of Easter. After feeling intense grief with Jesus in his last days of life on earth, we can enter with powerful gratitude into the moments when various disciples meet Jesus after his resurrection. Our thankfulness for the resurrection takes away our despair, but we can continue to hold our

---

[9] McKee.

feelings of sadness about Jesus' death in one hand, while we hold our joy in the resurrection in the other hand.

Even as Easter comes, and we rejoice with all that is in us about the gifts of the Resurrection, we don't forget the pain that Jesus experienced to get us to Easter. Without holding onto that grief in one hand, our joy would become saccharine, and our compassion would be obliterated.

The events of Holy Week can be juxtaposed with the Psalms, which lay out a pattern of grief and gratitude that gently oscillates between two poles. On the one hand, the Psalms contain mournful and passionate expressions of pain, sadness, anger, and grief, showing us that God invites us to bring those emotions into God's presence. Jesus' pain, sadness, and grief during his three years of ministry, intensified during the last week of his life, mirror many of the emotions expressed in the Psalms. But the resurrection enables us to say with the writer of Psalm 30: Yes, weeping may endure for the night, but joy almost always comes in the morning, and sometimes even sooner. Bringing our grief into God's presence enables us to receive joy in return.

In his life Jesus models honest expressions of both grief and thankfulness. The apostle Paul's letter and prayers model that combination as well. The Psalms and the New Testament give us patterns to follow as we try to overcome the powerful messages of our consumer culture and the lessons from our childhoods. Many forces hinder our honest expressions of grief, but with effort and conviction, we can learn to hold grief in one hand. Choosing gratitude day after day also requires an effort. Learning to hold grief in one hand and gratitude in the other will help us nurture compassion and wholeness in our challenging daily lives.

A Prayer

Jesus, Savior and Living One, we so often sing our praises to you for your death on the cross and your resurrection from the dead. Your love for us is beyond our imagining, and we cannot thank you enough that you loved us so much that you came to earth for us. Help us to experience the emotions of Holy Week with you and your disciples. Help us to grieve with you for the events of that week that are mirrored too often in events in our world today. Help us to be honest about our sadness while we rejoice and give thanks for your gift of love. Amen.

Questions for Discussion, Reflection, and Journaling

1. Which of Jesus' emotions during Holy Week stand out for you? Which of the disciples' emotions do? Can you identify some of the reasons those emotions seem real to you?

2. This chapter discusses three metaphors—Jesus referring to himself as a hen (Matthew 23:37), Jesus separating the sheep from the goats (Matthew 25:31–46), and the vine and the branches (John 15:1–17). The Holy Week narratives contain other metaphors, including Jesus' prayer about the cup passing from him (Matthew 26:39). In what ways do the metaphors of Holy Week speak to you of grief and gratitude?

3. The opposition of the religious leaders is visible in many ways during Holy Week, and Jesus directly addresses the heavy burdens they create for people (Matthew 23:4). Describe your grief and gratitude related to Christian leaders in your life.

4. Describe the ways you grieve about the betrayals by Judas and Peter and the ways you are thankful for God's forgiveness of human betrayal.

5. What do you think it looks like in practice to grieve the high cost of Jesus' death on the cross while also rejoicing in the resurrection?

6. Think of five things you are thankful for today, and spend a few moments thanking God for them. While you are praying, express to God any sadness you feel today.

Chapter 7 • Personal Reflections about Grief and Gratitude

Bless the LORD, O my soul,
and all that is within me,
bless his holy name.
Bless the LORD, O my soul,
and do not forget all his benefits—
who forgives all your iniquity,
who heals all your diseases,
who redeems your life from the Pit,
who crowns you with steadfast love and mercy,
who satisfies you with good as long as you live
so that your youth is renewed like the eagle's.
—Psalm 103:1–5

I am crying at 60 miles per hour. I have just dropped my husband, Dave, at a hospital in Bellevue, Washington, and I am driving back to our home in Seattle. The early morning view from the floating bridge crossing Lake Washington is gorgeous: the delicately tinged blue waters of the lake and the pink sky, with tall trees crowding the hillsides covered with houses on either side of the lake.

We are blessed to have access to good medical care, so Dave can have cataract surgery and get his sharp vision back. I am driving to our comfortable home, where I will eat breakfast; we have a place to sleep and food on the table. Before I pick up Dave later this morning, I'll work on my blog post for the week. I am so grateful to have meaningful work to do. Already a friend has texted to say she's praying for Dave's surgery. The friends and family members who support us are more precious than words can describe.

At the same time, the homeless population of Seattle is exploding. Yesterday Dave went downtown to the historic Pioneer Square area to finish a watercolor painting he started more than a year ago, and the view he had painted is now covered with a sea of tents, home to dozens of people experiencing homelessness. The delta variant of Covid-19 is still rising, and the earth's seas and temperatures are also still rising. Plastic still clogs the ocean and fills the bellies of sea birds and sea mammals. For a decade or two, we have talked about the rising income and wealth inequality in the United States, and the pandemic more clearly revealed such deep income and racial gaps. So many countries around the world are experiencing profound challenges, and so many people's lives are in turmoil. No one can agree on how to address these issues, and the disputes are vicious and destructive. My tears come from the juxtaposition of so many blessings and so many sources of pain.

The only other time I can remember crying at 60 miles per hour was in 2000, while driving from my brother's home in southwest Portland, Oregon, to the airport in the northeast part of the city. It was noon on a Saturday, and I was sailing along, looking forward to greeting a friend at the airport. I knew that in Seattle, at noon on a Saturday, everyone would be driving well below the speed limit because our freeways are so crowded. In that moment I felt that the constant traffic snarls we deal with in Seattle had robbed me of my city. I was and am profoundly grateful to be a Seattleite, with all our natural beauty and with so many supportive friends in "my" city. But in that moment on the freeway in Portland, I was overwhelmed with pain at the rising and frustrating traffic congestion we experience in Seattle far too often.

That memory of crying about too much traffic illustrates the complexity of life today. That moment in 2000 was before September 11, before the big economic downturn in 2008, and before the pandemic. When I cry now, the sources of sadness are multiple, never just one thing. The pandemic seems to have intensified my awareness of the many things I am sad about in my life and in our world.

The tears hurt. Grieving hurts.

Two years ago, when I discovered the quotation about holding grief and gratitude in two hands, it sounded like a life-giving practice. I dived into a series of blog posts about it, and I began to practice it in a small way. The more I practiced it, however, the more the grief portion of it hurt. And hurt. And hurt. Then Covid-19 hit, with all its socioeconomic disparities and political polarization, and the grief seemed to multiply and hurt even more.

I feel thankfulness and grief within my own body, soul, and spirit. I'm so thankful for the ways I've grown as a person over my lifespan, for the intellectual, emotional, and spiritual skills I've learned and gifts I've been given in those areas from God. But, oh my, how I grieve the self-absorption, anger, vindictiveness, jealousy, bitterness, gossip, and many other deep-rooted behaviors that sweep across my heart and mind, day after day, and that manifest themselves in my actions far too often. My own sins are part of the immense brokenness that made it necessary for Jesus to come to earth and die on the cross.

Humans have never been able to engineer a way to grieve that doesn't hurt. Yes, we can cover over grief with things like shopping, forced optimism, relentless activity, cookies, or alcohol. Many times in the past two years I have wondered whether that's perhaps what I should revert to. However, Christians have long pondered how to honestly approach God with grief. The basic principles of the Christian faith encapsulate grief and gratitude, and to deny the sources of human pain would deny the necessity for Jesus to come to earth.

The Book of Common Prayer, in Communion Liturgy C, summarizes our situation clearly:

> From the primal elements you brought forth the human race, and blessed us with memory, reason and skill. You made us the rulers of creation. But we turned against you, and betrayed your trust; and we turned against one another.
>
> *Have mercy, Lord, for we are sinners in your sight.*
>
> Again and again, you called us to return. Through the prophets and sages you revealed your righteous Law. And in the fullness of time you sent your only Son, born of a woman, to fulfill your Law, to open for us the way to freedom and peace.
>
> *By his blood, he reconciled us.*
>
> *By his wounds, we are healed.*[10]

The central message of Christian faith is rooted in grief and thankfulness: grief that the world is so broken that God had to send Jesus to earth and thankfulness that Jesus came.

Personal Responsibility for Things We Grieve

We grieve for the brokenness of the world that manifests itself in ways far from us but also in ways that we are personally involved in. Our level of responsibility varies related to the things we grieve, and our grief may take different forms related to the level of guilt that accompanies the grief. Consider these examples, which illustrate different levels of responsibility:

Grief example 1—A death far away. My husband's sister in Ohio died recently. I had nothing to do with her death, but I am grieving alongside her husband, her daughter and grandchildren, and my own husband. I experience sadness but no guilt.

---

[10] *The Book of Common Prayer* (New York: Seabury Press, 1979), 370.

71

Grief example 2—My fault! I can no longer walk for exercise because I have so many joint problems (hips, knees, feet) from osteoarthritis, which was caused by inflammation and obesity, both of which were caused, entirely or partly, by eating too much and especially eating too many inflammatory foods such as cookies and cake. For decades I loved walking and praying, a major source of both exercise and spiritual health, so my grief is intense when I think about not being able to walk very easily any more. I really wish I could have figured out something less damaging to do when feeling stress and pain than to eat cookies. In this example my grief is coupled with feelings of guilt, regret, and responsibility, an internal mess of thoughts and feelings.

Grief example 3—Challenging relationships. This example falls somewhere between the previous two examples. Sure, some of the people in my life are difficult. But in many instances, I can see that I am at least partly responsible for the challenges in those relationships. I can see moments when I don't have enough love, I'm not patient enough, and so on. Again, grieving about those relationships is coupled with other messy feelings of guilt, regret, and shame, but the guilt and shame are not too intense, because I can see a significant contribution by the other people to the relational challenges.

In the past two years of this journey with grief and gratitude, I've been paying attention to my inner dialog. Often my grief slides into self-criticism, as I replay events when I could have acted differently and perhaps warded off the thing I'm grieving now. I need to continue to learn how to grieve the event but also to grieve, and then let go of, the self-criticism.

Often when I replay past events, I criticize myself for my feelings of grief, especially in the light of so many things I'm thankful for. If I'm so thankful, then why aren't the thankful feelings enough to overcome the grief? This is a replay of messages from childhood and the wider culture. I need to continue in my journey of learning how to grieve, then let go of, my self-criticism for not being optimistic or thankful enough to ward off grief.

Sometimes the sadness feels like a bottomless pit, and I fall into the very common belief that if I let myself grieve, it will never end, and I will be sucked into permanent darkness and depression. I need to return again and again to the Psalms with their rhythm of grief and gratitude, sadness and praise.

Lingering in Thankfulness

In the summer of 2021, during the writing and editing of this book, our refrigerator began to smell oily when we opened it, and a thick black film began to appear on everything in the fridge. We have a small dorm fridge in our basement, so we brought it upstairs, ate as much food from the big refrigerator as we could, and crammed the rest of the food into the little fridge. Because of labor shortages, it took a month for a repair person to come. He said the fridge could not be fixed.

I looked around for a fridge in stock in a store in Seattle. I was so happy when I found one that would fit into the hole in our kitchen designed for the refrigerator. However, the salesperson gave me a delivery time two and a half months later! I asked if I could be put on a list for earlier delivery in case of a cancellation, and it still took more than a month to get the new fridge.

The absence of a regular-sized fridge for more than two months, and the presence of that little dorm fridge, caused so many unexpected forms of thankfulness. I was grateful that we owned the dorm fridge, so we didn't have to use coolers and ice. What a blessing that we had the money to buy the new fridge. The tiny size of the dorm fridge made me so much more intentional about what I bought at the grocery store and what I cooked, forcing me to think more about the privilege of buying food, which led to more gratitude for the simple but enormous gift of eating three meals a day.

I so often chafed that I couldn't cook a big batch of soup and eat it for several days in a row. That chafing made me so grateful that for my entire adult life, I have had a reasonably large fridge, and I have been able to cook and store large batches of food. I had no idea how essential a large fridge is to my pattern of life, and I will never take one for granted again. I have laughed at the astonishing number of times each day the absence of a large fridge has impacted our lives. The connections between laughter and thankfulness have become more visible. How many people experience a dorm fridge as a call to laughter and thankfulness? That makes me laugh again.

The lightness that thankfulness can bring has been an enormous gift in the pandemic. In the past, thankfulness for me has so often been connected with negative self-talk. "Why do you feel so sad about things when you have so much to be thankful for?" Affirming the significance of both grief and gratitude, held separately in my two hands, has helped me let go of some of that self-talk, and the things I'm thankful for bring much more joy and laughter. Thankfulness used to have a hook of guilt attached to it, because it was never enough to conquer sadness and grief. Now thankfulness is more often connected to joy and laughter, a wonderful gift.

The Juxtaposition of Grief and Gratitude Is Everywhere

"I see grief and gratitude in Nehemiah," my husband tells me one morning after he has been studying the Bible. He points out the many sources of grief in Nehemiah's time, right after the exiles returned to Jerusalem: the wall is being rebuilt so slowly, Jews have adopted the worship patterns of local people, and over and over the people of Jerusalem fall into a cycle of sin and idolatry. One of the big events in

Nehemiah is the first Feast of Tabernacles celebrated after the exiles have returned to Jerusalem. The festival helps them remember the years in the wilderness after being freed from slavery in Egypt, a vivid celebration of God's faithfulness. God has never forgotten the people of Israel and will never forsake them. More than two millennia later, as we read the story, we grieve at the sin of the people, and we give thanks for God's faithfulness to them.

In the two years I have been trying to hold grief and gratitude in two hands, I have seen the pattern my husband identified. I see it woven throughout the Bible, and you have read some of those patterns in this book. Increasingly I see it in daily living. So many things evoke thankfulness: lacy trees, the scent of flowers, delicious food, gentle touches, a deep sleep, a fleeting moment of joy, beautiful art, lively music, a treasured possession, the memory of a wonderful vacation, a birthday gift, a stimulating conversation, and on and on. Yet so many events, people, and bodily aches make me sad. So much of this happens every single day.

Sometimes I don't want to be mature, as Francis Weller recommends. In some ways my life was better when I buried all sadness with cookies, ignored many of the small blessings of life, and got on with the tasks that needed to be done. I could ignore so many sources of pain. However, I now see the pattern of grief and gratitude woven throughout the Bible, and I experience the benefits of honesty before God. I find so much more joy in God's gifts to me, small and large. Sources of grief and gratitude have become impossible to ignore, and holding them in two hands helps us grow in honesty, authenticity, peace, and joy.

A Prayer

Compassionate God, you know. You know how hard honest grief is for us. You know how much it hurts. You know how often we are tempted to cover over our sadness with activity or consumption. Teach us to lament, honestly and openly, in your presence. Beautiful God, you know. You know that we have moments when our hearts our lifted by this intricate world you created. You know we have moments of deep gratitude for so many components of our daily lives, and you also know how hard we find it to stop and pay attention to your gifts. Teach us how to practice thankfulness, day after day, and enable us to laugh with you at the joy of your wonderful gifts. Help us walk with Jesus in sadness and joy, and in lament and thankfulness. Amen.

Questions for Discussion, Reflection, and Journaling

1. After reading this book, what new patterns do you see from your family of origin about grief and gratitude? In what ways are those patterns still influencing you today? What would you like to change?

2. What do sadness and grief look like in your life? Where are they located in your body? What are some of the thoughts that often accompany sadness for you?

3. During the pandemic, what did you grieve the most? What were you most thankful for?

4. Where do you see the connections between laughter and thankfulness for you? Do you have inner messages that keep you from enjoying the lift and joy of thankfulness? How might you pray for God's help in changing that?

5. Think of five things you are thankful for today, and spend a few moments thanking God for them. While you are praying, express to God any sadness you feel today.

6. Write or say a prayer about what you have learned about grief and gratitude from this book. What are you thankful for that you have learned or thought about in a fresh light? What do you want to ask God for?

Acknowledgements

I am so grateful for Beth Gaede and my supportive husband, Dave Baab, both of whom gave me help with copy editing and proof reading. I am indebted to Carol Simon, who gave me feedback that resulted in a change in structure of this book. Lynne Taylor also made helpful suggestions about content. To each of you, many thanks.

I want to express my thanks to all the people who have listened to me talk about my sadness and anger throughout my life. So many individuals have cared for me in the midst of hard things and challenging times. God has been merciful to me through you, and I have not grieved alone. Thank you.

Books and Bible Study Guides by Lynne M. Baab

Visit my website at lynnebaab.com to learn about these books. You can also access many articles I've written, as well as weekly blog posts.

Nurturing Hope: Christian Pastoral Care in the Twenty-First Century, 2018

A Garden of Living Water: Stories of Self-Discovery and Spiritual Growth, 2017

Death in Dunedin: A Novel, 2015

The Power of Listening: Building Skills for Mission and Ministry, 2014

Deadly Murmurs: A Novel, 2013

Joy Together: Spiritual Practices for Your Congregation, 2012

Dead Sea: A Novel, 2012

Friending: Real Relationships in a Virtual World, 2011

Prayers of the New Testament. A LifeGuide Bible Study Guide, 2010

Prayers of the Old Testament. A LifeGuide Bible Study Guide, 2010

Reaching Out in a Networked World: Expressing Your Congregation's Heart and Soul, 2008

Sabbath: The Gift of Rest. A LifeGuide Bible Study Guide, 2007. (Titled *Restoring the Sabbath* in the U.K.)

Fasting: Spiritual Freedom Beyond Our Appetites, 2006

Sabbath Keeping: Finding Freedom in the Rhythms of Rest, 2005

Beating Burnout in Congregations, 2003

A Renewed Spirituality: Finding Fresh Paths at Midlife, 2002

Embracing Midlife: Congregations as Support Systems, 1999

Personality Type in Congregations: How to Work with Others More Effectively, 1998

For Further Reading

Diana Butler Bass. *Grateful: The Subversive Practice of Giving Thanks*. San Francisco: HarperOne, 2018.

C. S. Lewis. *A Grief Observed*. San Francisco: HarperOne, 1961 and 2009.

Eugene Peterson. *Answering God: The Psalms as Tools for Prayer*. San Francisco: HarperOne, 1991.

Soong-Chan Rah. *Prophetic Lament: A Call for Justice in Troubled Times*. Downer's Grove, IL: IVP Books, 2015.

Oliver Sacks. *Gratitude*. New York: Knopf, 2015.

Jerry L. Sittser. *A Grief Disguised: How the Soul Grows through Loss*. Grand Rapids, MI: Zondervan, 2004.

David Steindl-Rast. *Gratefulness, The Heart of Prayer: An Approach to Life in Fullness*. Mahwah, NJ: Paulist Press, 1984.

Ann Voskamp. *One Thousand Gifts: A Dare to Live Fully Right Where You Are*. Nashville: Thomas Nelson, 2011 and 2021.

Mark Vroegop. *Dark Clouds, Deep Mercy: Discovering the Grace of Lament*. Wheaton, IL: Crossway Books, 2019.

Printed in Great Britain
by Amazon

25303508R00046